Blacks

A Diopian View - on Anthropology, Religion, and Afrikan and European Civilizations - From Prehistory to the Modern Era

By John (Yohana) Striggles, B.A. M.S.

Reprinted July 2014

Cover design by CustomWebOnline.com

BK Royston Publishing
P. O. Box 4321
Jeffersonville, IN 47131
502-802-5385
http://bkroystonpublishing.com

© Copyright 2014 – BK Royston Publishing LLC

All Rights Reserved. No part of this book may be reproduced, stored in a retrieval system, or transmitted by any means without the written permission of the author.

Published by: BK Royston Publishing LLC
Cover Design by: Customwebonline.com
Layout by: BK Royston Publishing LLC

ISBN-13: 978-0692242421 (BK Royston Publishing)
ISBN-10: 0692242422
LCCN: 2014911332

Printed in the United States of America

The Foreword
Some Reasons for this Manuscript

Let us begin by quoting the master Black historian Yosef A.A. ben-Jochannan:

> No man forever allows his Mother, which is the Land of His Origin, to be constantly subjected to all sorts of vilification without one day rising to the challenge; even if it means his eventual annihilation, for that has been man's historical behavior.
>
> If the European Jews can fight for an arid piece of desert; the Irish for a small emerald island; the British for a barren island of misery; Protestant Anglo-Saxon Americans for their stolen 'Indian' empire; why should the Black man (the African, African-Caribbean, and African-American) not fight for the richest piece of real estate on the planet earth—his original homeland— 'Mother Africa' (Alkebu -lan)? He must, though the struggle seems at times insurmountable. For it is in the doing of the impossible which made the Blacks and African great for hundreds of centuries....[1]

Culturally conscious Black men must struggle; it is our only option to assert ourselves as whole and independent beings. Y.A.A. ben-Jochannan's provocative quotation above is sufficient encouragement to state that the culturally and technologically equipped Black man must prepare to repatriate himself; that is, the culturally and technically prepared Black man must migrate to Afrika to participate in its building and industrialization. Black men (and women, of course) should also consider that no self-respecting person covets or steals that (e.g., the stolen "Indian" empire called the United States of America) which belongs to another.

This manuscript is humbly submitted to aid in the decaucasianization of Black people. With that in mind, let us hear from another master Black historian Chancellor Williams:

> Nothing is clearer than the tragic fact that Africa, like the rest of the Black world, has only the illusion of being free and independent. It is still as economically enshackled as it ever was—in some respects even more so. The study of this period [1950 to the present] and the conditions it presents will confront Blacks of the world with the final challenge. The response to that challenge will be the test of the genius of the race. The outcome and indeed, the whole future of the race, depends upon the extent to which we have become intellectually emancipated and decaucasianized enough to pioneer in original thinking.
>
> Those who do become free in fact, will no longer readily grab the white man's ideologies and systems whether Capitalism, the Western version of democracy, or Communism--without a critical review and analysis to determine whether Africa's own traditional system, when updated, may not be truly superior and best fitted to meet the aspirations of the Black world. This last period, then, is the time of great decisions. It may well be the Black race's last chance for a rebirth and salvation.[2]

With the physical and psychological salvation of Blacks at stake, it is obvious that historical texts about Blacks should not be submitted as purely intellectual or academic endeavors.

> The status of African people throughout the world remains too precarious to deal with their history by merely chronicling important events. The situation demands that greater efforts be made to determine the meaning of those events, their effect on the people, the overall change in the direction of history, and what new directions the race must take.³

The supreme Afrikan historian-scientist Cheikh A. Diop concurs with the preceding opinion of Chancellor Williams:

> Intellectuals ought to study the past not for the pleasure they find in so doing, but to derive lessons from it or, if necessary, to diseart those lessons in full knowledge of the facts. Only a real knowledge of the past can keep in one's consciousness the feeling of historical continuity essential to the consolidation of a multinational state.⁴

The genius that he was (deceased), C.A. Diop also espoused the consolidation of the Afrikan nations into one political unit or federation.

Given the promptings by great Black historians, it is the further aim of this author to combat Negrophobia in full knowledge of the facts; this Negrophobia being committed by Westerners/Europeans/Caucasians (and Negroes themselves) against Blacks.

At this point, it is necessary to give special attention to the multi-genius Cheikh A. Diop, whose Two (Geographical-) Cradles Theory undergirds this entire manuscript:

> Cheikh Anta Diop (in <u>The African Origin of Civilization</u>) has a theory that there is a basic global division of peoples into two kinds [of culture]: the NegroAfricans and the Aryans--a category for

whites. An Aryan is either a Semite (Jew or Arab), a Latin (from Europe or South America), a Nordic (from Germany or the U.S.A.), or a Slav (whether in Russian or in Canada).[5]

Nations Negres et Culture is the most audacious book that a Black man has ever written up to this point, according to Aime Cesaire, the profoundly brilliant Martinician politician, poet and playwright.

The final part of Nations Negres et Culture, Paris Presence Africaine, 1955, dealt with the industrial prospects of the African continent. Diop felt that these prospects were 'perhaps the most important, because they must be realized first so that we may all the better achieve the others. It is by industrialization to the utmost that we shall obtain the material power necessary to guarantee our political frontiers.' (Taken from Le Congres de Writers et Ariste Noire, Presence Africaine, 1957, p. 353.)

... all Africans should be forced to realize "the industrial destiny of Africa and the need for her sons to equip themselves for the tasks which await them."[6] *Diop*: "We must be armed to the teeth with science to go to reconquer our cultural inheritance. This is the task which awaits the future generation."[7]

At this time, I will briefly interrupt my focus on C.A. Diop to restate emphatically the main reason for this document: Blacks must struggle to liberate themselves and their original homeland; that is, Blacks must prepare themselves culturally and technologically to be repatriated--to return to Afrika to participate in its rebuilding and industrialization. Actually, what I have just stated coincides nicely with Diop's dream that all of Afrika's sons (and daughters!) arm themselves scientifically to reconquer their cultural and physical inheritance. To be explicit, it is the intent of your author to follow his own advise or die trying! Having made myself as clear as possible, allow me to add the voice of the Black giant Malcolm X to this discussion:

> If we [the Organization of Afro-American Unity] are extremists, we are not ashamed of it. In fact, the conditions that our people suffer are extreme and an extreme illness can not be cured with a moderate medicine. We're not against the physical migration of our people back to Africa. Those who want to go back and have something to contribute to the development of Africa, we are for them ....[8]

Let us now return to the profound cultural philosophy of C.A. Diop, as explicated by James Spady:

> Upon closer examination it may be proven that Diop's thinking during the early 1950's can be favorably compared to Franz Fanon, Kwame Nkrumah, Aime Cesaire, and Sekou Toure. There is one central theme which flows through all of Diop's works. It is the concept of cultural unity which is a synthesizing factor. Culture for Diop is a weapon in the battle for African liberation.

> Cheikh Anta Diop's concept of cultural unity is the most important contribution to African Historiography since Ibn Khaldun.[9]

It is especially interesting to note that worldly scholar Ibn Battuta—a 14th century contemporary of Arab historian Ibn Khaldun—was a black man, according to Afrikan historian J.C. de-Graft Johnson, despite his Arabic name. [**Author's note**: Scholars (such as Cheikh Diop, Said Hamdun and Noel

King) who have translated Ibn Battuta's 14th century narratives differ with de-Graft Johnson. They identify Ibn Battuta as an Arab.] This would not be an insignificant example of the process of being culturally and linguistically dominated. Afrikans that are linguistically colonized are more difficult, if not impossible, to identify among the pages of history by their Black posterity. This point has been amply taken by Chancellor Williams, in his crucial work The Destruction of Black Civilization. But, now another quick example of the cultural philosophy of C.A. Diop:

> Consequently, the Black man must become able to restore the continuity of his national [Afrikan] historic past, to draw from it the moral advantage needed to reconquer his place in the modern world ....[10]

The reader of this text will note, obviously, that I have quoted liberally many historians and scholars, most of whom are Black. It has not been my intention to paraphrase the historians quoted herein; in my opinion, the best effect is achieved when these masters speak directly. Returning to the Black historian James Spady and the cultural philosophy of C.A. Diop:

> It was important for Cheikh Anta to speak on the origin of cultural differences between Europe and Africa. For it's only through learning the historical background of those differences that one is able to chart our future.[11]

With my present understanding of Afrikan history, I would say that the lesson to be learned about the irreconcilable cultural differences between Europeans and Afrikans

(Blacks) has been accurately summarized by the Black mental giant Malcolm X, in the following:

> Don't let us [Blacks and Whites] try and mix because every time that mixture takes place we always find the Black man low man on the totem pole.[12]

Indeed, the destruction of Blacks and their civilizations (or High-Cultures) is the lesson to be learned from the mixing of the irreconcilable Aryan and Afrikan cultures, respectively. This lesson of history was documented to the nth degree by the late Chancellor Williams, in his vital work The Destruction of Black Civilization. It should follow that the additional aim of this writer and text is to emphasize the destruction of Black people by Europeans and white Asians (e.g., the Arabs) and their respective cultural institutions.

Preface

In 1990 at age 39, I wrote Blacks, after independent, African studies beginning in the 1970s. I self-published in order to share my new-found knowledge with others; I had written Blacks to satisfy my personal curiosity and need for greater self (and group) knowledge. As such, the caustic tone of my writing then was not profane, but it is very likely considered "politically incorrect" in the 21st-century United States by the dominant group, or white Americans.

Nevertheless, it behooves me to make a brief comment about one target of my strident language in this Second Printing of Blacks.

Throughout the book, the reader will see my reference to Western capitalism and its effects on the world and Africa, specifically. It seems obvious now that the last 500 yrs of world history have born witness to the rise of Western nations and their version of capitalism.

Nevertheless, as I presently understand it, capitalism is simply the monetary difference (excess, surplus) between the cost to manufacture a good or service and the price at which that good or service is sold. Therefore, it can be understood that "capitalism" is inherent (and necessary) in any monetary transfer of goods and services between individuals and countries, if the manufacturer is to derive a living from the sale of his or her product.

Thus, the reader should understand that my negative references to Western capitalism in Blacks are directed at hyper-capitalism, or the host of capitalistic transactions taking place between individuals and countries that have resulted in the impoverishment of people.

On the other hand, with respect to the traditional African system, monthly meetings from 2005-2012 with Indiana Univ.-Southeast sociologist Dr. Ben Asare have made me aware of the morphing of traditional chiefs in Ghana into quasi-feudal (land) lords, something retrogressive economically-speaking. (See "Urbanization and Agricultural Development," by Ben Asare, Temple University, 1986.)

Also, for any reader of my second book Too Late to Go Home? (2013) it will be obvious that I have learned increasingly over the years (including an almost two-year residence in Africa) of the psychology of black (African) people that negates their group autonomy and self-control, the actions of others (whites, Arabs, etc.) of the past ~5,000 years notwithstanding.

Furthermore, since completing Blacks in 1990 and writing of Arab, historical incursions into Africa, I have been informed of former Arab leader Col. Moammar Gadhafi's efforts to assist all of Africa avoid Western telecommunications domination. In the 1990s, Col. Gadhafi infused $300 million into RASCOM—Regional African Satellite Communication Organization—so Africa would have its own satellite(s) and control communication costs on that continent.

It is worth noting also that South African legend Nelson Mandela traveled to Libya and thanked Col. Gadhafi for his monetary and military support of the black struggle in So. Africa during that country's white apartheid era.

Otherwise, the 21st century has seen Arab attacks in present-day Sudan continue until blacks of southern Sudan have been forced to separate and form the new nation (republic) of South Sudan in 2011.

John (Yohana) Striggles

2014

(P.S. In keeping with the original spirit of Blacks, the use of upper-case letters is used to denote the races, in spite of recent, grammatical convention.)

Table of Contents

Foreword ....

Preface……………………………………………....

Chapter 1	Paleoanthropology and the Origin of Blacks and Whites	1
Chapter 2	Ancient Egypt's Gift to the World - Civilization and the Caucasian's Northeast Afrika Syndrome	13
Chapter 3	The Ancient Greek and Roman Experience: Individualism, Patriarchy, and a Stolen Legacy	45
Chapter 4	The Afrikan Origin of Religious Thought and the Major Western Religions: Judaism, Christianity, and Islam	67
Chapter 5	Major Western Religions and the Destruction of Afrikan Civilizations	91
Chapter 6	The Glory of Medieval, or Precolonial (Pre-European), Black Afrikan Nation-States and their Destruction by Arabs and Europeans (and European-Americans)	117

Chapter 7	A Comparison of Political and Socio-economic Structures in Europe and Precolonial Black Afrika	141
Chapter 8	A Poem for Black Minds	171
	Endnotes	173
	A Brief List of Articles and Pamphlets Consulted ...	193
	A Partial List of Works Consulted	199
	Bibliographies	205
	Chart A: Cheikh Diop's Two Cradle Theory	211

Chapter 1

Paleoanthropology and the Origin of Blacks and Whites

Humanity came to life, was born, at the source of the Nile Valley, in the region of the Great Lakes (in central-east Afrika).[1] That profound statement is of the greatest significance to contemporary Blacks and their descendants; it is the starting point from which to create the new (redeveloped) Afrikan personality. That humanity that was born at the source of the Nile Valley was Black; that is, all humanity was originally Black. The truth about the location of the origin of Black people (from whom Yellow and White peoples evolved at a much later date), at once, brings Afrikan history into direct conflict with the mythic and ambiguous biblical (see the book of Genesis) description of the Mesopotamian location of the origin of humanity (i.e., the mythical Adam and Eve).

The study of paleontology aids to dismiss the biblical (Old Testament, specifically) fallacy and Negrophobia about the location of the origin of humanity. It is interesting and necessary to note that the Bible (and the Koran!) serves as a function of White cultural imperialism and Negrophobia, as does the polygenetic (multi-genetic) theory of the evolution of the human races.

> The polygenetic theorists tried to establish a hierarchy of races and to indicate that some races are inferior to others. But if man has the same origin, then there can be no intellectual hierarchy, because all races, the three races of the world, would have the same intellectual history.[2]

In the Descent of Man, [Charles] Darwin reasoned that 'in each region of the world, the living mammals are closely related to the extinct species of that same region. It is therefore, probably that Africa was formerly inhabited by extinct apes closely allied to gorillas and chimpanzees; and as these two species are now man's nearest allies, it is somewhat more than probable that our early progenitors lived on the African continent than elsewhere.' Apart from the apparent disconcerting conflict [between biochemists and paleontologists] over the time-scale of human evolution, studies do emphasize very cogently the human relatedness with chimpanzees. For instance, A. Wilson with MarieClaire King, has compared the structure of many proteins in humans and chimpanzees. The difference they find is a small one: 99 percent of their protein structure is the same. Even if there were no fossils to back up Darwin's perceptive claim for an African origin of the human race, Allan Wilson and M.-Claire King's results would be powerful support by themselves, as chimpanzees are exclusively African animals. By this [protein structure] test, chimpanzees show closer relatedness to humans than to Asian apes. For instance, according to molecular calculations, the hominid, chimpanzee, and gorilla lines separated from the ancestral stock four million years ago; the orangutan about seven million years ago; and the gibbon, ten million years ago. [Biologists] Vincent Sarich and Allan Wilson do not dispute the 'order' in which apes turned off into their own specialized paths, but they do suggest that it all happened much more recently than the paleontologists believe.[3]

As the original race, Blacks are the source of whatever intellectual capacity that exists today among the Black, Yellow, and White races, respectively. Humanity came to life, was born, at the source of the Nile Valley, in the region of the Great Lakes [in central-east Afrika]. We are discussing a crucial period in prehistory (i.e., before written records), when Black people were the only race on the face of the earth; it will be hundreds of thousands of years before the appearance of the Yellow or White races. This period of history should inspire an infinite number of questions in the Black mind, e.g.: How and when did the Yellow and White races evolve from the Black race? Since Blacks were the only race on earth for at least 1.5 million years, the whole host of societal and technical devices necessary for group living are the sole creation of Black people, e.g.: family relationships, speech, tools, the control of fire, etc.

Is it obvious to the reader that Blacks can increase their self-esteem by claiming an endless array of prehistoric inventions? It is imperative that the redeveloped (historically conscious) Afrikan personality reject White cultural imperialism in the form of the Bible (and the Koran!), since a biblical chronology does not acknowledge the vast achievements of Black people during prehistory.

I shall return to our observation of the Black race, as it develops during the Stone Age period of prehistory.

We can fix the origins of humanity at 5.5 million years ago. This humanity comprised six specimens. The first five have disappeared completely.... The three final specimens did leave Africa; the first which was Homo Erectus went into Europe 400,000 years ago, he went into Asia 500,000 years ago. he was followed by what we call Neanderthal Man and then followed by Homo Sapiens-Sapiens. It is in the region of Kenya where we find all the most ancient evolutionary information. No other continent in the world has a complete series of fossils indicating the six specimens. The three specimens that represent the very beginning of mankind cannot be found in Europe, they cannot be found in Asia, ... They never left Afrika![4, 5]

We can establish that 120,000 years ago this later man [Homo Sapiens] ... existed in Africa. He was only in Africa for a very long time, and not on any other continent. He lived in Africa at least until 40,000 years ago before he left Africa. During this time no other part of the world was populated by man like us [i.e., Black Homo Sapiens-Sapiens].[6]

... Homo erectus made its appearance, around one and a half [1.5] million years ago. This large-brained ancestor [Homo erectus] of ours (it has a brain size of about 900 cc) was living alongside the lake [East Turkana in Kenya] about one and half million years ago. The loss of thick body hair probably happened at an early stage in the development of 'Homo erectus' in Africa.

Increased pigmentation must probably have arisen at an early stage of Homo erectus while

> still in Africa. The need protect the skin through pigmentation arose as early hominids [Homo erectus] lost thick hair covering.[7]

The preceding quotations intimate the significance of paleontologists; that is, social (and physical) scientists draw conclusions about a race from which that respective race then forms an image of itself. It, therefore, behooves Black people to stay abreast of all the academic disciplines which may affect their self-image and subsequent self-esteem.

It is necessary to pause to consider the psycho-genetic effect of pigmentation or melanin. I am aware that a number of Black physical and social scientists explain the xenophobic (war-like) behavior of Whites as a result of the absence of melanin; likewise, these Black scientists explain the xenophilic (peaceful; accepting) disposition of Blacks as a result of the abundance of melanin. These Black scientists argue cogently that the worldwide oppression and murder of Blacks (and people of color) by Whites (including the innumerous burnings, bombings, lynchings, and castrations in the U.S.) is a direct function of the relative inability of Whites to produce melanin. I would strongly urge the Black reader to pursue the literature on melanin, especially Dr. F. Cress Welsing's works including her <u>Cress Theory of Color-Confrontation and Racism</u> (1970).

> Melanin is directly associated with the proper functioning of the central nervous system which is essential to human sensitivity and consciousness. Relationships have been found to exist between melanin and the reticular formation and melanin and the red nucleus. Parkinson's disease, largely confined to whites, is associated with the loss of melanin-pigment by cells of the substantia nigra in the mid-brain. PKU disease (hereditary idiocy),

like Parkinson's disease, is more common among whites than Blacks.[8]

I am returning to the Old Stone Age period of prehistory, 120,000 years ago, when Black Homo sapiens (i.e., modern man) represented the only race on the face of this planet. The Black reader must understand that I am not examining the evolutionary record as a purely intellectual endeavor. It is extremely necessary for Blacks to study the evolution of the Black race in order to understand the circumstances under which the White race was born, since the existence of this race has proved fatal to Black people. Needless to say, Black people must reject Western religious chronologies (in the Jewish Torah, Christian Bible, and Muslim Koran, respectively) since those chronologies (and their Negrophobic Ham myth) do not provide a rational explanation for the origin of the Black, Yellow, and White races, respectively. If it interests the reader, I shall examine the ridiculously Negrophobic Ham myth of the Bible (the book of Genesis) in Chapter five. Now, onward to pinpoint the birth of the lethal White race.

> More than 150,000 years ago, beings morphologically identical with man of today were living in the region of the great lakes at the sources of the Nile and nowhere else. From the Upper Paleolithic [Stone Age] to the dynastic epoch [in ancient Egypt], the whole of the Nile river's basin was taken progressively by these Negroid [Black] peoples.[9]

> Discoveries made by Dr. Verneaux and a group of French scientists and archaeologists in southern and western France and Italy show that from 30,000 to 40,000 years ago the population of these regions was Negroid

[Black] in features.[10] The Grimaldi, a Negro [Black] people that inhabited Europe about 15,000 to 25,000 B.C., were the first known artists. The Venus of Willendorf, a statuette of a negro woman, said to be the oldest representation of the human form in existence and now in the Vienna Museum, is attributed to the Grimaldi Negroes. Grimaldi carvings have also been found in North Russia. Two complete Grimaldi skeletons are now in the Museum of Monaco, in the Riviera (France), where they were found.[11] At best, it has been possible to extract with more or less certitude, the existence, at this far distant period, of a fertility cult, thanks to the discovery of the steatopygous statuettes (the Venus of Willendorf and others) whose area of dispersion extends from W. Europe as far as Lake Baikal in Asia and to Japan. The presence of a southern Negroid [Black] element in So. Europe during the Aurignacian [an Upper Old Stone Age period characterized by a particular tool culture] Age is confirmed by the presence of the Grimaldi Man.[12]

It is from 40,000 to 20,000 years ago that Grimaldi man left Africa to go into Europe at the time of the last glaciation. During this period of some 20,000 years, he underwent an adaptation to become what we know as the white man.[13] As people [Black Grimaldi men] moved into colder climates, pigmentation [melanin] would have become a disadvantage.... Because the people [Grimaldi] living in Europe some twenty thousand years ago were battling with ice-age conditions, they generally retreated to caves, where they could escape the worst ravages of the cold.[14] Europe was slowed down by glaciation—it was frozen! Glaciation stopped about 12,000 years ago. It is only at that time that European expansion will start....

It was so cold in Europe [during the final glaciation] that it was not possible to live on the open ground, it was necessary to live in caves. He [Grimaldi man] came to Europe 40,000 years ago [Black Homo erectus had come before Grimaldi man and disappeared]. Between 40,000 to 20,000 [b.c.e.] it [Grimaldi man] changed and gave birth to ... Cro-magnon [White] man. So for 40,000 years, it's only Grimaldi man that existed throughout the world.[15] ... If mankind originated in Africa, it was necessarily Negroid [Black] before becoming White through mutation and adaptation at the end of the last glaciation [12,000 b.c.e.] in Europe in the Upper Paleolithic; and it is now more understandable why the Grimaldi
Negroids [Blacks] first occupied Europe for 10,000 years before CroMagnon Man--prototype of the white race--appeared.[16]

At any rate, ..., before 20,000 B.C. there were no whites in existence. There is absolutely no doubt that the white race which appeared for the first time during the Upper Paleolithic--around 20,000 B.C.--was the product of a process of depigmentation. Yellows appeared even later, around 10-15,000 B.C. Today, science can rely on irrefutable material evidence to illustrate these facts.[17]

Given the current conditions of Black people throughout the world, present-day Blacks might well wish that their early ancestor (i.e., Grimaldi man) had never been so inquisitive and brave as to venture from Afrika into Europe, to become entrapped during the last glacial period, where he mutated into the White (Cro-Magnon) man. If the fossil record provided by archaeology and paleontology were not sufficient to render an evolutionary explanation of the origin of the three races, the scientific disciplines of biochemistry and genetics could offer additional proof. It is biologically impossible for whites to produce offspring of color; that is, it is genetically possible for Blacks to produce relatively albino (White) offspring, while, the opposite is genetically impossible.

Pinpointing the origin of the White race is crucial to understanding a premise underlying this entire text: It is the 1,000s of years that Whites spent isolated in their cold and barren geographical home (Europe) that has shaped their individualistic, acutely materialistic, warlike, and patriarchal traits. As we shall see in the following chapters, these respective European (Aryan) traits would prove fatal to Blacks and all Afrikan civilizations, beginning with the invasion of ancient Egypt by barbaric White nomads.

Apparently, the search for one's (individual) familial genealogy has become the most current cultural fad among Negroes in America. However, by utilizing the disciplines of paleontology and physics, Blacks can reinforce the cultural (racial) unity and consciousness of all Black people by examining the peopling of Afrika starting from the ancient Nile Valley; that is, the Nile Valley is the original location of the genetic pool from which all present-day Black families sprang.

Probably in prehistoric times, the northern part of the Empire of Ghana was populated by folk coming from South Africa and the region of the Great Lakes. Indeed no trace of the paleolithic [Old Stone Age] is found in W. Africa; the only place where it has been found with certainty is at Pita in Guinea; south of the Sahara, in general only the Neolithic ["New Stone Age"] is to be found, while in the Sahara itself are to be found all the periods of prehistory.[18] The first Nigerian civilization [named the Nok civilization] ... has been traced back to the first millennium B.C., the ceramics found there being radiocarbon-dated over a range from 900 B.C. to 200 A.D. We now know, thanks to radiocarbon methods, that the earliest sites of Zimbabwe do date back at least as far as the first century of the Christian Era.[19]

In W. Africa, one can be certain only that Neolithic remains are attributable to tall Blacks. The Paleolithic (remains) are, generally speaking, of uncertain age: some are found at Pita, in Upper Guinea. Testimony converges to prove that in the fifth century [400] b.c., on the whole, tall Blacks had not yet peopled W. Africa. When So. African populations are questioned, they say they came from the North; those of the Gulf of Benin say they came from the Northeast. In antiquity, the Ethiopians called themselves 'autochthonous' those who had sprung from the ground. In all likelihood, after the drying of the Sahara [ca 7000 b.c.e.], Black mankind first lived in bunches in the Nile basin before swarming out in successive spurts. One could thus localize in the Nile Valley coming from the Great Lakes, the primitive cradle of all Black peoples today living dispersed at various points of the continent.

In Africa, totemic clan names are, to an extent, an ethnic indication; .... Lists of comparative proper [totemic] names give an idea of how the African continent was peopled. Starting from the Nile basin in successive waves, the populations radiated in all directions.[20] The grammatical relationship between the African languages of today, such as Walaf, and ancient Egyptian of the 18th dynasty [ca 1580 b.c.e.] ... shows that the comparison of the two realities far from being illusory, is legitimate....[21]

Chapter 2

*Ancient Egypt's Gift to the World - Civilization and the Caucasian's
North-east Afrika Syndrome*

(For the Anderson and Franklin Families and the Memory of
Keith Larue, Joe Miller, Sr., and Amani Shule)

The master Black historian Chancellor Williams has stated that the rebirth and salvation of the economically and psychologically dependent Black race rests in its decaucasianization and the subsequent decisions Blacks make about their aspirations. It should be understood that Black people have been culturally caucasianized. That idea is not difficult to understand: Black slaves were stripped of their Afrikan culture (original language; crafts and professions; historical knowledge, heroes, and pride; etc.) by their European masters and were, thereby, eventually transformed into Negroes (i.e., Blacks who deny being Afrikan in favor of being an American). Lest Black people forget, the Arabs (White Asians) have and continue (see present-day Sudan and No. Afrika) to oppress (kill) Afrikans, in the same tradition as Europeans.

Let us witness the tool of cultural domination (imperialism) as utilized by Whites against Blacks.

> The historian J. Henrik Clark points out how Europeans have maintained their control of our past: 'History was written or rewritten to show or imply that Europeans were the only creators of what could be called a

civilization.'[1] The negation of history and of the intellectual accomplishments of Black Afrikan people is cultural and mental murder which has already taken place and has paved the way for genocide here and there in the world.[2]

Champillion, the Younger [1790-1832 c.e.], further advanced the false theories of a white Egypt. He states: 'The opinion that the ancient population of Egypt belonged to the Negro African race, is an error long accepted as the truth.'[3] Since then [1820 c.e.] the succession of dishonest Egyptologists, armed with a very determined scholarship, have perpetuated a crime against science which is known, by subscribing to a deliberate falsification of human history. Upheld by all of the Western [European] countries, ... The new Egyptological ideology, born at the opportune moment was used to support the theoretical bases of imperialist ideology. It was propagated with the aid of extensive publicity and taught globally.[4] Materials that come from digs that have already been done are in different European museums. Hundreds of thousands of mummies have been destroyed. The criteria of choice, of what had to be kept and what had to be destroyed, those criteria were established by foreign [White] minds whose interests it was to whiten Egyptian civilization. But they [Whites] have tried to take the foreign types that lived in [ancient] Egypt at the time and make people believe

that those foreign types were the actual
Egyptians [Blacks].[5]

European cultural imperialism (domination) has followed both military (the Afrikan slave trade; colonialism and the partition of Afrika) and economic imperialism as the means to control the minds and resources of Black people. Even given the aim of White cultural imperialism to subjugate the mind and actions of Black people, a curious Black might wonder still about the special and prolonged 165 year effort of Aryan scientists and scholars, through lies and distortion, to whiten ancient Egypt (and the rest of No. Afrika!). In an effort to properly describe the obsession of White academicians and historians to whiten ancient Egypt, I have borrowed a phrase from Dr. Y.A.A. ben-Jochannan, i.e., "the White man's North-east Afrika syndrome." Ancient Egypt was the pinnacle of the world's first civilization (high-culture) and was created by the Nile Valley Afrikans. It was this ancient Black civilization that presented the arts and sciences to the entire world, beginning with the Greeks (Achaeans) who were so barbaric and nomadic that they might have remained steeped in barbarism forever had it not been for ancient Egyptians.

To support the idea made manifest by European military imperialism that it is the fate of Afrikans to be ruled economically by Whites, Western Egyptologists have exhibited their North-east Afrika syndrome to whiten ancient Egypt. While I shall go on to list a few of the ancient Egyptian achievements that White historians have been so anxious to claim, I would especially like the Black reader to be aware of a basic premise important to this text: The Nile River Valley imposed peculiar physical conditions upon Blacks and is responsible for Blacks developing a collective, settled mode of life and specific psychosocial traits; likewise, the cold and barren European landscape (steppes) imposed particular physical conditions upon Whites and is responsible for them developing a individualistic, nomadic existence and specific psycho-social characteristics (those characteristics exist to this day!).

> Contrary to a current belief, [ancient] Egypt was not that land hidebound by a religiosity that prevented it from conquering nature through science. Let it be remembered that it was this country, which through science brought mankind out of prehistory to the real conquest of civilization.[6] It has been determined, in fact, by means of astronomical calculations, of mathematical precision, that in 4,241 b.c. a calendar was in use in Egypt.[7] The discovery that the helical rising [i.e., rising simultaneously with the sun] of Sothis [the Dog star] coincided with the annual twelve months, each consisting of thirty days, with five extra days added to keep the calendar in step with the seasons. This Sothic year, which was inaccurate by only one-fourth of a day, appears from reliable calculations to have been inaugurated on July 19.... Both by its character and its role in history, the Nile is unique among rivers; it has shaped man's ideas to a greater extent than any other purely terrestrial phenomenon. The rise and fall of its waters have been as a pulse to quicken his mental development, even while they sustained his life from season to season.[8] Ancient Egypt's astonishing architecture surpassed all the other nations that have existed upon earth.[9] The Egyptian cult of the dead [ancestor worship] stimulated the building of the first buildings in dressed stone.[10] When in perfect condition, the one

and one-half mile avenue between the Temples at Luxor [Wo'se] and Karnak was the most extraordinary the world has ever seen.[11] To Imhotep, the architect-minister, is attributed the invention of columns, an invention which makes the heavy stonework look light and graceful.[12]

The [ancient] Egyptians invented algebra. The Egyptians were the first to invent trigonometry. Problem 56 [of the Rhind Mathematical Papyrus] involves the calculation of the incline of a pyramid, which is the same as calculating a tangent. Speaking exclusively of what is certain, one must say that the Egyptians have passed down to posterity the formula of the exact surface area of the sphere [$4(pi)r^2$] and the exact 'formula' of the volume of the cylinder [$V=(pi)r^2$], calculated with the value of pi = 3.16. In actual fact, the whole corpus of Egyptian mathematics does not include a single erroneous formula be it in geometry, in algebra, in trigonometry, in arithmetic or in mechanics: therefore, it can only be a highly theoretical science.[13]

According to Homer [ca 881 b.c.e.]: 'In Egypt the men are more skilled in medicine than any of human kind.'[14]

Who, then in the 20th century, would believe that these same Blacks were of the race that built great cities, developed writing, the arts and sciences when the whites of Europe were still roaming tribes of barbarian warriors? ... How then explain the descent of Blacks from the heights reached by their forefathers to the depths in which they find themselves today?[15]

The Black is clearly capable of creating technique. He is the very one who first created it at a time when all the White races, steeped in barbarism, were barely fit for civilization. When we say that the ancestors of Blacks, who today live mainly in Black Africa, were the first to invent mathematics, astronomy, the calendar, sciences in general, the arts, religion, agriculture, social organization, medicine, writing, technique, architecture; that they were to first to erect buildings out of six million tons of stone (the Great Pyramid) as architects and engineers — not simply as unskilled laborers; that they built the immense temple of Karnak — that forest of columns with its famed hypostyle hall large enough to hold the Notre Dame Cathedral in Paris with all its towers, the Greek Parthenon could fit into those walls even more easily (Greco-Roman monuments are mere miniatures as compared with Egyptian monuments); that they sculpted the first colossal statues (Colossi of Memnon, etc.) ... Black Africans can and must exclusively lay claim to the cultural heritage of old Egyptian civilization. They are the only one today whose sensitivity is able to blend easily with the essence and spirit of that high culture which Western [White] Egyptologists find so hard to understand. The intellectual and affective dispositions of present-day Blacks are the same as those of

> the people who edited the hieroglyphic texts of the pyramids and other monuments and sculptured the bas-reliefs of the temples.[16]

Given the host of accomplishments attributed to the ancient Egyptian (Kemite) civilization, it is little wonder that European historians have tried for the past 165 years to whiten and claim that Nile Valley high-culture. Interestingly enough, this Caucasian tradition of intellectual dishonesty and trickery has its origin among the ancient Greek scholars and philosophers; I shall examine this character flaw of the ancient Greeks in the following chapter. To avoid being confused additionally about their heritage, Blacks must be aware that the Arab inhabitants of present-day Egypt (the United Arab Republic) are not the original or rightful occupants of that land. In 641 c.e., the avaricious (greedy) Arabs conquered Egypt and began to displace Blacks as the rightful inhabitants.

With the current psychological and economical dependency of Blacks upon Whites, it is paramount that Black people reclaim the great achievements of the world's original civilization (ancient Egypt), as part of the process of rebuilding their self-esteem and a national Afrikan historic-consciousness. That redeveloped historical consciousness can provide the conceptual basis for uniting all Afrikans, while, at the same time, provide Blacks with the intellectual independence to separate themselves from the psychological "tit" of their present-day Caucasian masters.

I am compelled to present a physical basis and rationale for defining the Ta-Merrians (ancient Egyptians) as black. I shall not belabor the point, since the racial identity of the Kemites (ancient Egyptians) has been proven many times by Black scholars.

> 'I would only mention that the Egyptians were Africans or coloured people, ... about the

same as you see the coloured people of the United States at the present day.... [David Walker's Appeal, 1829]'[17] The evaluation of the melanin level by microscopic examination is a laboratory method which enables us to classify the ancient Egyptians unquestionably among the Black race. Strabo [a Greek historian, ca 58 b.c.e. - 25 c.e.] visited Egypt and almost all the countries of the Roman empire. There is no doubt whatever as to Strabo's notion of the Egyptian's race for he seeks elsewhere to explain why the Egyptians are darker than Hindus, a circumstance which would permit the refutation, if needed, of any attempt at confusing the Hindu and Egyptian races.

There are about nine centuries between the birth of Aeschylus and Herodotus [the Greek father of Western history, b. 484?] and the death of Ammianius Marcellinius (33-100 c.e., a Latin historian and friend of Emperor Julian), ... during which the Egyptians, amid a sea of white races, steadily crossbred. It can be said without exaggeration that in Egypt [before the 6th century b.c.e.] one household in ten included a white Asiatic or Indo-European slave (Egyptian notables like to have a Syrian or Cretan female slave in their harems.). It is remarkable that, despite its intensity, all this crossbreeding should not have succeeded in upsetting the racial constants. Indeed Ammianus Marcellinus writes: '... the men of Egypt are mostly brown or black with a skinny and desiccated look.'[18] ... Ammianius, a ... [ancient] historian, says of the Egyptians of his time, 'Homines autem Aegyptt plerique subfusculi sunt et atrati (The men of Egypt are, as a rule, somewhat swarthy and dark of complexion).'[19] The Latin term 'fuscus' [i.e., dark, black] was interchanged with 'Ethiopian' ["burnt-face" as translated from Greek by the great Black historian John G. Jackson].[20]

I did not bother to add the observations of other eye-witness ancient Greek historians (e.g., Herodotus and Diodorus Siculus) to those given above; those Greeks attest plainly to the blackness of the ancient Egyptians (Kemites). I would maintain that any ignorance of Blacks to the information contained in this text is a function of the White cultural indoctrination inherent in Caucasian institutions (e.g., schools, the media, entertainment industry, etc.) and, of course, the lack of independent Black institutions. It is a frightening indication of the stagnation of the Afrikan, historical intellect or memory that contemporary Blacks are ignorant of the racial identity of the creators of civilization, when Black people (e.g., David Walker) living 160 years ago during the Afrikan slave trade were already historically conscious. If Negroes (i.e. Black people who reject their Afrikanity) were not so caucasianized, they could ask themselves why the descendants of the creators of civilization should be psychologically and economically dependent upon the barbaric descendants of the White race to whom the ancient Blacks originally taught the liberal arts and sciences?

I shall proceed to cite some Negrophobia and facts concerning the origins of agriculture and civilization. the great Afrikan historian John G. Jackson explains that the systematic growing of crops (agriculture) is a cultural activity which distinguishes man from the apes. It is a fact that agricultural irrigation was a specialty of the Ta-Merrians (ancient Egyptians). Perhaps the Black reader can appreciate the need of Aryan scholars to participate in the system of White supremacy by concealing the knowledge that the ancestors of Black people are the originators of civilization (including agriculture) and that those ancient Blacks taught the elements of civilization (e.g., domestication of other animals, weaving of clothes, metal working, and pottery making, according to J.G. Jackson) to the nomadic Caucasians who were so barbaric they had been unfit for civilization. How better to keep Afrikan people trapped in a state of psychological dependence than to conceal from them their grand cultural heritage (inheritance) and, thereby, rob them of the necessary incentive to disentangle themselves from the strangle hold of a world-wide White supremacy system in which economic exploitation reigns supreme?

> Civilization is the result of a long social process, which takes place in the same spot and is handed down from one generation to another, each one profiting by experience of the last.[21] The invention of agriculture was, without exaggeration, the most significant event in the history of mankind.[22] We know that 17,000 years ago, people on the African continent [in the then fertile Sahara] had started the domestication of plants [i.e., agriculture][23] At the time of the last Ice Age [the last Ice Age stopped about 12,000 years ago] in the northern hemisphere, the climate of Mediterranean countries changed; no rain fell in North Africa and the country began to dry up. The people [Blacks who had previously farmed the Sahara] had to move away [to the Upper Nile River] to find a steady water supply.[24] In Egypt, a dwarfish type of Negro [the Twa Blacks] seems to have inhabitated the Nile delta some 10,000 years

ago; and big black Negroes [Blacks] formed the population of upper Nubia [present-day Sudan] and Dongola as late as about 4,000 years ago.[25] The Badarians, a Negroid [Black] people, who inhabited Upper Egypt about 6,000 b.c. are said to be the first to pass from the stage of hunting to agriculture and stock-breeding, thereby taking the first step that led to our present civilization.[26]

[Negrophobia:] In any event it [agriculture] began in many areas, though perhaps the most favored locality was the fertile crescent [the TigrisEuphrates River Valley] around the southeast edge of the Mediterranean, ...[27] In the beginning [in Mesopotamia], ca 3000 b.c., three regions could be distinguished: ancient Elain [Elam] or Susiana; Sumer with Our its capital; and Akkad, the capital of which was Agade.

The Mesopotamian history of the early millennia is not well-known. Sumerian history presents one important particularity; the whole of its first period is known only through inferences drawn from the [Babylonian] Code of Hammurabi (ca 2100 b.c.). The language of the city-state of Sumer was neither Semitic, Indo-European, nor Chinese. The oldest period of Sumerian [Mesopotamian] civilization is alleged ... to go back to 3000 b.c. to make it coincide with the very beginning of Egyptian history.[28] Moreover, apart from some stations of uncertain age in Palestine, no trace of man earlier than 4000 b.c. exists in Syria or Mesopotamia [the

TigrisEuphrates River Valley]. By that date [4000 b.c.e.] the Egyptians had their feet on the threshold of their [written] history proper. Nowhere else do we find a Chalcolithic [copper tools] industry comparable in its technical perfection.[29]

The Negrophobic remark examined above is a product of the world's foremost White paleoanthropologist. One would think that he knew better than to ambiguously suggest that the fertile crescent area of ancient Mesopotamia, of which Sumer formed the earliest civilization, was the most likely locale for the origin of agriculture. Interestingly, through the late historian-philosopher-physicist-Egyptologist C.A. Diop destroys properly the Negrophobic notion of Mesopotamia and Sumer being the origins of civilization and agriculture, respectively, we are told by historian J.G. Jackson that the Sumerians are described in ancient inscriptions as the "blackheads" or "black-faced people." There is profound irony here: While White scholars conspire to move the origin of high-culture (civilization and agriculture) away from Afrika to a rather vague location in Sumer (Mesopotamia), these same Negrophobes avoid crediting the creation of civilization to one group of Blacks (ancient Egyptians) in favor of bestowing (unbeknowingly?) that achievement upon another group of Blacks (Sumerians).

I am proceeding to discuss some facts and Negrophobia concerning the discovery of iron smelting (metallurgy). The physical evidence of removing iron from its ore (rock) with a primitive furnace in central Afrika has been dated to ca 47,000 b.c.e. Iron metallurgy is another element of civilization which the ancient Egyptians (Ta-Merrians) transmitted to the entire Old World. The practical product of iron smelting is hard metal tools capable of maintaining both an edge and a point necessary to chisel and shape stone into permanent buildings and fixtures. For example, J.G. Jackson informs us, via the ancient historian Herodotus, that iron tools were used by the ancient Egyptians in building the Great Pyramid.

> 'The production of iron was the event of events in human ... experience, without a parallel, and without an equal, beside which all other inventions and discoveries were inconsiderable, or at least subordinate.'[30]
>
> The Letters of Armana are the remains of the administrative archives of the Egyptian chancellery after the conquest [a defensive reflex] of Western Asia by Thutmosis 3 in the 18th Dynasty. More than 110 states, including the Aegean Sea Islands, were conquered. At the time of [Pharaoh] Amenophis 3 [ca 1405-1370 b.c.e.], Phoenicia (Syria) was part of the Egyptian empire .... How can we so glibly talk about an autonomous invention in these regions in that period? The invention of iron metallurgy (by the so-called Hittites, for example) or so-called Phoenician writing is an abuse of speech. These Letters of Armana were the centralizing information of all sorts that Egypt collected at this time from these small states. The 'famous' Hittites were under the Egyptian protectorate. One can hardly imagine today the efficiency of the Egyptian administration of that time in ... [Western] Asia. ... Because of the Letters of Armana, it is thought that [iron] objects could have been offered to the Pharaoh or to one of his predecessors by some Asian sovereign. We know from what came before that they [the Hittites] were not even mentioned in history when we have evidence

of the [iron metallurgical] process in Egypt and, even more, they all were in varying degrees under Egypt's sovereignty at the time that one makes them inventors.

According to the same author (Prof. J. Leclant), the lump of stratum iron found at Abydos (6th Dynasty [2420-2270 b.c.e.]) could be a product of accidental fusion. On the frescos of the tombs of Rekhmire, vizier of [Pharaoh] Thutmosis 3 [ca 1504-1450], one sees blacksmiths using the same type of bellows used in Black Africa.... No accidental fusion made by an unskilled metallurgist of the protohistorical period would have led to iron exempt of carbon, i.e. soft and mild iron. An accident such as the one that Profs. R. Mauny and J. Leclant talk about is technically and scientifically impossible. The whole metallurgic technique consists in knowing what to do to diminish carbon. As a consequence, all the objects in soft iron recorded in Egypt are of high importance for metallurgic history.... The metallurgic process used by the Egyptians of the Ancient Empire [ca 3200-2270 b.c.e.] as attested by chemical analysis is the one that modern science in the [European] industrial era used to extract iron from ore.[31]

From Nubia to Senegal, active blast furnaces produced the iron required for technological and economic activity. Mining of ore, the smelting of metal, and working with it were not taught to Africans by any foreigners. In classical [ancient] times, Nubia (Meroe) was comparable to Birmingham [of British industry fame] in metallurgical production and distribution. The repeated victories of Nubia [led by Queen Candace!] over the Roman army [of Augustus Caesar led by General C. Petronius] in 29 b.c.e. may perhaps give us some idea of the technological level of Nubia [ancient Ethiopia which is present-day Sudan] in this period.[32]

By this time, the astute (observant) Black reader should not be surprised at the attempts of contemporary White historians to steal the achievements of protohistorical and ancient Blacks, in an effort to prevent the development of a strong Afrikan historic personality that would seek to separate itself from the fatal tentacles of the White supremacy (capitalist) system. Ironically, we are informed by the late Chancellor Williams that a grand and technical invention (iron smelting) the ancient Egyptians taught to the Old World would return (in 671 b.c.e.), in the form of superior iron weapons (swords) wielded by the Assyrians (White Asians), to conquer and ravage the Egyptian civilization itself. Since I am about to discuss the psycho-social traits of the ancient Egyptians and Ethiopians (Ta-Nahasi), I must mention briefly that the Egyptian military reflex, cited previously, will be explained later in this chapter; the Letters of Armana, cited previously, are only the result of the ancient Egyptians' counterattack and selfdefense maneuver against the bellicose (warlike) Western Asians.

The psycho-social makeup of the ancient Egyptians and Ethiopians was identical; as a matter of fact, ambassadors to-Egypt for the ancient Ethiopians told the Greek historian Diodorus Siculus that they were the cultural and biological ancestors of the Egyptians. Even more, the psychic disposition of ancient Afrikans is identical to that of Blacks today. That statement can be deduced, if the Black reader understands a basic premise of this text as formulated in C.A. Diop's Two Cradle Theory: It is the tens of 1,000s of years that Blacks spent isolated and developing in their mild and fertile geographical base (Afrika) that shaped their collective, peaceful, xenophilic (accepting), and matriarchal traits.

> Most of us [Blacks] are not even equipped to systematically refer to the Nile Valley for an understanding of either present day or ancient structures of our society. Yet, we can make very little headway in understanding our cultures, languages, and social structures without a thorough knowledge of many facets of ancient Egyptian civilization. Ancient black Egypt was in every sense the actual cradle of our cultures. Without a systematic reference to Egypt, there can be not true cultural renaissance in Africa [or among Afrikans in the diaspora].[33] Far from being a diversion centered around the past, a look toward ancient Egypt is the best way to conceive and build our cultural future. Egypt will play the same role in the rethinking and renewing of African culture that ancient Greece and Rome play in the culture of the West [Europe and European-America].[34]
>
> The Old [Egyptian] Kingdom [ca 3200-2270 b.c.e.] had been a period of almost uninterrupted political, social, and artistic development.[35] Although private enterprise was permitted and even encouraged, ... the fact is that the governance of a relatively large [Nile River Valley] territory with local

dignitaries and great projects subordinated the individual's quest for individual advancement.[36] If we may believe the eulogies which the Egyptians who followed Ptahhotep (the Grand Vizier under King Issy [during Dynasty 5, ca 2565-2420]) inscribed upon their tombs, it was an age [Dynasties 1-6, ca 3200-2270; or Dynasties 1-10, ca 3200-2100 b.c.e.], and perhaps the first age, in human history when, men were consciously striving to attain righteousness. His [vizier Ptahhotep's] cardinal recept he might have taken from the Memphite text (the so-called Memphite Drama which dates from the 1st Dynasty [ca 3200-2980 b.c.e.] and is the oldest written record of human thought) itself:

> 'Great is righteousness; its dispensation endures, nor has it been overthrown since the time of its maker (the sun god, Ra) for punishment is inflicted on the transgressor of its laws.... Although misfortune may carry away wealth ... the power of righteousness is that it endures.... Make righteousness to flourish and thy children shall live.... Established in the man whose standard is righteousness, who walketh according to its ways.'.[37]

In a governor's tomb [during Dynasties 4-5, ca 2680-2420 b.c.e.] at BeniHassan, the following inscription can be read:

> I oppressed no widow. No farmer was sent away unheard. No shepherd was turned away ... in my district nobody suffered from hunger, nobody grieved. When years

of famine came I caused the land to be ploughed and so I kept my people alive. I did not favor the high above the low. When years of abundance came I did not ask for taxes still due.

The following comes from literary inscriptions left by King Amen-enhet [Dynasty 12, ca 2000-1979 b.c.e.] as good advice for his son Senwosre 1 [1970-1936 b.c.e.] on how to rule the country:

'Listen to what I have to tell you, So that you may augment that which is good.

I gave to the beggar, And took care of the orphan, I was accessible to the idlers, And also to those of importance.'[38]

Until the time when the Southern world [Afrika] was menaced and invaded by the Indo-Europeans [Aryans], during the second millennium [1675-1600 b.c.e.].[:] 'Numbers of the Egyptian sovereigns seem to have lived peacefully and the frequent eulogies of peace, almost in modern tones, constitute not the least remarkable oddity in even the official literature of Egypt.' Before the attacks of the Northerners [Whites], war was not a prerogative of the South [Afrika], neither was agriculture that of the North [Eurasia]. The king of Egypt was indeed the hawk god Horus, living for the greatest benefit of all even in his sporting activities: 'Hunting and fishing, he still carries out his conventional role of sovereign, since he always shows himself in so doing, skillful, strong, and careful, while hunting at least--even crocodiles and hippopotami existed in the swamps--to clear the country of wild animals.'[39]

Unlike other cities in the ancient world (Babylon [in Mesopotamia], for example), there were no surrounding walls at Memphis.[40] It was after having been subjected to these first invasions [by White Asians from ca 1675-1600 b.c.e.] that Egyptians, particularly, raised fortifications, at the gates of their country, as at Sinai [i.e., ancient Memphis or present-day Cairo]. Nubians [ancient Ethiopians] and Egyptians of antiquity felt very comfortable in their own country and did not wish to leave it; they were not conquerors.[41]

A.J. Arkell, Early Khartoum: An Account of the Excavation of an Early Occupation Site Carried Out by the Sudan Gov. Antiquities Service in 1944-45, 111-14, points out (a) that the early Khatoum [ancient Ethiopia, present-day Sudan] people belonged to a Negroid [Black] whose pottery and barbed stone spears seem in type to predate the earliest known in Egypt and that it is reasonable to think that they may have been passed onto predynastic [pre 3200 b.c.e.] Egypt; (b) that the tradition preserved in Diodorus 3.2.1-4 of the southern origin of many Egyptian customs may contain some truth.

Homer tells us that the Olympians [Greek gods] were fond of visiting the Ethiopians. Zeus, followed by all the gods, went to feast with the blameless Ethiopians, where he remained for twelve days. Ethiopians, as Diodorus [of ancient Sicily] had said ... were the first to honor the gods. Aelain [an ancient Greek author] does not overlook the fact that Ethiopia is the place where the gods bathe. To Dionysus 'Periegetes' the Ethiopians were godlike and blameless. The Ethiopians, according to Stobaeus, practice piety and justice; their houses are without doors and no one steals the many things left in the streets.[42]

Turning to Taharqa [an ancient Ethiopian king] as one of their own, rebellious Egyptians, according to Assyrian king Ashurbanipal (669-626 b.c), sought the Napatan [Napata was a capital of Ethiopia] king's assistance in freeing Egypt from Assyrian domination.... In other words, Taharqa was a native son, not a foreign invader like the Assyrians [Whites]. The Napatans [Ethiopians] of the Twenty-fifth Dynasty appeared to Egyptians in many respects as native rulers rather than as foreign invaders.[43] The remarkable stele of the Ethiopian King Piankhi (ca 751-716 b.c.) found at Gebel Barkal [in Ethiopia] records his conquest of Egypt [Piankhi recaptured Egypt from White Libyan usurpers] and shows in scrupulous attention to religious ritual, respectful of temples and the gods of Egypt,.... Herodotus wrote that Sabacos [Shabakha], of the Ethiopian [25th] Dynasty [ca 718-653 b.c.e.], when King of Egypt never put to death Egyptian wrong-doers but instead required them, according to the severity of their offense, to contribute to civic improvement by raising the embankments of their cities. Concerned lest he commit sacrilege, Sabakha, in the Herogotean account, voluntarily retired from Egypt, after he had been terrified by a dream that he would assemble all the Egyptian priests and put them to death.[44]

The abundance of Ethiopian food resources is symbolized by what Herodotus and legend call the 'Table of the Sun.' At sunrise, any of the people could profit from the food provided freely and anonymously. Prisoners were secured by golden chains. The material reasons which kept the Ethiopians in their birthplace and prevented them from becoming conquerors can be understood. In fact--according to Herodotus--when Cambyses conquered Egypt (525 b.c.) he wished to cross the Nubian desert but nearly lost his life there. Through [Ethiopian] representatives Cambyses was lectured in the following terms: 'The King of the Ethiops thus advises the king of the Persians--... let him thank the gods that they have not put it into the heart of the sons of the Ethiops to covet countries which do not belong to them. According to the same author [Herodotus] the respect of the individual was such that when a Nubian was condemned to death, he was ordered to destroy himself at his own house. If then he tried to leave the country secretly, Herodotus [the ancient Greek father of Western history] says that it was his own mother who watched over him and took upon herself the duty of [putting him to death before he could carry out his plan.[45]

A word needs to be issued to prevent the reader from being confused. The land referred to an ancient Ethiopia is the present-day Sudan nation; present-day Ethiopia is the ancient land of Punt. The conquest and destruction of ancient Ethiopia and its eventual mutation into modern-day, Arab-controlled Sudan should be instructive to Blacks. It reveals a more than one thousand year effort to steal the land of Afrikans. To bolster their self-respect, it is necessary for Blacks to know that the ancient Ethiopians fought greatly to maintain the integrity of their territory. In order to sustain Black legitimist rule in ancient Egypt as well as their own land, the Ethiopians fought, variously, beginning in the 8th century b.c.e. until the 19th century c.e., the following Whites: Libyans, Assyrians, Persians, Greeks, Romans, and Arabs (including the Ottoman Turks).

Through the Two Cradle Theory lengthily examined in his various encyclopedic books, C.A. Diop explained why the psychic disposition of ancient Afrikans is identical to that of Blacks today: It is the tens of thousands of years that Blacks spent alone and developing in their mild and fertile geographical base (Afrika and the Nile Valley specifically) that molded their collective, xenophilic (peaceful, accepting), and matriarchal traits. If that is so, the material which follows immediately is of specific interest to the Black female reader, since it begins to show the privileged status that Afrikan women held in ancient Black society. This special consideration, given Afrikan women by Black men, can be compared in the following chapters with the disregard and deprivation received by White women at the hands of White males of ancient yesteryear and today.

> The sacred character of the mother in societies which are sedentary and matriarchal is ill-suited to the idea of a primitive stage of promiscuous intercourse which they could be said to have passed through. It also seems that the women even played in important role in

the discovery of agriculture and in plant selection while the man devoted himself to the hunt. In ancient Afrika, women took part in public life and had the right to vote and enjoyed legal status equal to that of men. Ancient Egyptian women went about freely and unveiled unlike some Asian [Islamic; Hindu] women.[46]

'... The matriarchal system, on which the [ancient Egyptian] family was based. All landed property descended in the female line from mother to daughter. When a man married an heiress, he enjoyed her property only as long as his wife lived. On her death, it passed to her daughter and her daughter's husband ... which explains why so many Pharaohs married ... even their infant daughters. Often these marriages were purely formal affairs. The throne went strictly in the female line. The great wife of the king was heiress; ... The king's birth was not important ...; the queen was queen by right of birth, the king by right of marriage.' The custom of matrilineal descent also explains the many marriages of Cleopatra [an Afrikan-European]; .... When Julius Caesar [a Greek general] took Egypt, the only way by which he could be acknowledged as ruler was by marriage with the queen....[47]

Up until the end of Egyptian history, the people [the masses] remained monogamous. Only the royal family and the court dignitaries practiced polygamy, in varying degrees, depending on their wealth. This appeared to a

> luxury granted on to family and social life, instead of being the primordial [original] foundation of it.
>
> In Africa: including Egypt and Ethiopia, the woman enjoyed a liberty equal to that of a man, had a legal individuality and could occupy any function ([e.g.,] Candace, Queen of Ethiopia and commander of her army). She was already emancipated and no public act was alien to her. Matriarchy ... is a harmonious dualism, an association accepted by both sexes, the better to build a sedentary society where each and everyone could fully develop by following the activity best suited to physiological nature.[48]

It is to be seen, from the preceding quotes, that political and material rights were transmitted (and continue to be transmitted today in non-Westernized Afrika) through the female. This method transmits political rights according to uterine consanguinity or uterine kin. It shall be evident in the following chapters that the position of females in White society has been completely opposite to that of Afrikan women in Black culture.

The ancient queen Cleopatra (a mulatto [Black] born of Afrikan and Greek parents) was indeed an Egyptian woman, through whom political and social rights were granted. Though her reign in Egypt (ca 30 b.c.e.) is insignificant, except that it exposes the powermad psyches of the Greeks and Romans, she has become, nevertheless, an object of European-American Negrophobia, as expressed by the film and television industries, etc. That is, White females have been used to portray ancient Black women, in a disingenuous (dishonest) attempt to conceal the racial identity of the original Egyptians. Can the Black reader guess why and from whom the lessons of ancient Egypt and No. Afrika are being concealed?

In the reference material quoted above, the reader will notice that a minority (1 in 10 households) of the ancient Egyptian population, the nobility, practiced polygamy. Previously, in this text, it has been stated that various Pharaohs (e.g., Pepi I of Dynasty 6, ca 2270, and Una of Dynasty 7) enjoyed having a Caucasian female in their harem. This infatuation with Indo-European females as exhibited by the Black nobles was by no means the ancient Afrikan norm; however, it can be compared strangely with the behavior of some modern-day Negro males and their preoccupation with Caucasian females. Still, there is a severe distinction between the Egyptian noble's infatuation and the contemporary Negro's godlike adoration for White females. The following references (quotes) will illustrate how the Afrikan trait of xenophilia (the love and acceptance of strangers) and the effort of Blacks to integrate Whites into ancient Egyptian civilization proved to be its downfall.

> As early as the Eleventh Dynasty, Blacks, Whites, and yellow-skinned men lived in Thebes [Taiba], just as there are foreigners residing today in Paris [France]. The choice of coloring [of the front of the respective deceased's coffin] shows that in Thebes, under the Eleventh Dynasty [ca 2100-2000 b.c.e.], yellow, white, and black men lived, were accepted as fellowcitizens, and admitted into the Egyptian necropolis.[49]

> Thebes was full of foreigners, Semites, Libyans, and Achaeans [protoGreeks], as Byzantium was to be later at the time of the Byzantine Empire [i.e., the East Roman Empire].

'It was even reduced to defending its territory, its past, and even its language, against these foreigners who presented themselves as friends, allies, or servants, and who infiltrated it peacefully.... It remained the most celebrated and richest city in the world; this city [Thebes in Upper Egypt] of gold still attracted the attention and the covetousness of the Achaeans.... How many are the Achaean [proto-Greek] nobles who must, ..., have gone there and spent long months and long years in this capital of civilization.'[50]

After the arrival of the Hyksos [1675-1600 b.c.e.], the first walls were seen around Kemite [Egyptian] cities.[51] Egypt only became a conquering and imperialist nation by reaction, by self-defense after the occupation of the Hyksos [white Asians, Indo-Europeans], under the Eighteenth Dynasty; particularly under Thothmes 3 who is often called the Napoleon of Antiquity. For this seventeen [17] expeditions were required. This victory [the 8th expedition] assured him the subjection of those great warriors the Assyrians, the Babylonians, and the Hittites, who all paid tribute to him. On the eighth expedition, he left Egypt by sea and landed in Phoenicia [Canaan], had boats built at Byblos and had them carried across the desert to the Euphrates River, which he was thus able to cross and defy the Mitanians.[52]

[Indo-European] tribes had attacked Egypt and were defeated. This is 1300 b.c. There were [tens of] thousands of prisoners who were branded with an iron, with a letter, that meant that they were slaves. They were distributed around, in the different temples in Egypt. They were transformed into farmers.[53] A thousand years after the arrival of the Libyans [barbaric Whites who lived on the fringes outside of Egyptian civilization] in Afrika, they were still nomads, Herodotus describes how they were scattered around Lake Tritonis in Cyrenaica and as far as the outskirts of Carthage [modern-day Tunisia].[54]

From the Nineteenth Dynasty [ca 1340-1212 b.c.e.], in virtually each Egyptian family, there was a foreign slave. In virtually all Egyptian families there were white slaves. It is in that manner that Egypt started to have mixed races.[55] In fact it was the whole of Egypt which received an increasingly important flood of foreigners of the Achaean [proto-Greek] race. Every time the Pharaoh conquered the 'peoples of the sea [White nomadic invaders]',

> 'he spared the survivors, enrolled them, and distributed them throughout his construction yards or in his military outposts. They became the best [?] workers and best [?] soldiers of the king....
> '... Domiciled or quartered in barracks in Thebes and in the Provinces, these mercenaries married Egyptian women, mixed with the population, became respectable people and even important personages attaining honours and riches.

Under the twentieth dynasty (1200-1100 b.c.) in Thebes itself a good part of the officers and officials were Syrians and Berbers of recent adaptation.'[56]

Pharaoh Thotmes 3's [18th Dynasty, ca 1504-1450 b.c.e.] armour-bearer, Meri-Re and his brother, priest User-Min, were Amorites. A Semitic general named Yanhamu, mentioned in the Tel-Armana letters [ca 13701352 b.c.e.] as governing the Egyptian domains in Palestine, was not the first Palestinian to hold high office under the Pharaohs.[57] After the death of Rameses 2 [ca 1298-1232 b.c.e.], Egypt declined rapidly mainly because of the inertness and the lack of national spirit possessed by the hosts of foreigners [Whites] who lived there and Egypt became a mart and a home of traders instead of warriors.[58]

Rameses 3 [ca 1198–1168 b.c.e.], the son of the powerful king Seth-akht who began Dynasty Twenty, reorganized the army and introduced conscription. The wonderful temple of Medinet-abu in Thebes was built for Rameses 3. On its lofty walls are depicted his military expeditions [at least five major battles against invading Indo-Europeans] and these tell of the gigantic struggle that this last really great Pharaoh made to prevent the breakup of his mighty empire. When Rameses 3 established peace, he devoted energy to the government of his empire. He promoted trade, improved irrigation, and saw to it that those who served him in the army and navy were well trained. Ships were refitted and well armed, and soldiers were adequately paid.

Rameses 4, son of Rameses 3, was the first of a long line of weaklings who reigned over Egypt. He did one noteworthy thing; he made a list of all his father's achievements, and this scroll, a papyrus twenty-nine [29] yards long, is of the greatest importance. It was placed in his tomb.[59] After the New Empire [ca 1600-1090 b.c.e. Dynasties 17-20], Egypt will decline. The highest point of Egyptian history was the Nineteenth dynasty of Rameses 2.[60] [Pharaoh] Psammetichus 1 [a white Libyan, ca 663-609 b.c.e.], Dynasty Twenty-six, was considered by the people [Blacks] as a usurper who delivered Egypt 'to the dregs of the nations', to foreigners, by facilitating their installation. In particular, he surrounded himself with Greek mercenaries and conferred upon them the highest civil and military posts in the court. That was when garrisons of the national Egyptian army, out of frustration and as legitimists (this was a part of the army composed of loyal citizens), went to place themselves at the disposal of the king of Nubia ([present-day] Khartoum, Sudan). They numbered 200,000 and were assigned to the region between [present-day] Bahr-el-azrek and Bahr-elabyad. They multiplied and become the 'automoles' mentioned by Herodotus [an ancient Greek historian].[61] Greek mercenaries, perhaps Egyptian-born and children of the mercenaries who had served under the earlier Psammeticus [1], had been employed by Psammetichus 2 [ca 594-

588 b.c.e., Dynasty 26] in his Nubian campaign; inscriptions at Abu Simbel [Nubia; ancient Ethiopia] record the participation of Greek mercenaries in the campaign.[62]

I have examined, thus far, two Afrikan civilizations and, already, a fatal pattern emerges: White people have destroyed each Black high-culture in which they appeared. That fact should not surprise the Black reader; in recent years, scholars such as Y.A.A. ben-Jochannan, Chancellor Williams, H. Madhubuti, Bobby Wright, and Sterling Plumpp (too name just a few) have been working and writing endlessly to bring to the attention of Black people the tendency of Whites and their cultural institutions to annihilate Afrikan culture. Whether the warlike, xenophobic traits of Indo-Aryans result from the 1,000s of years they spent isolated in inclement Europe (as Dr. C.A. Diop reasoned), or, whether those destructive traits result from white melanic deficiencies (as Dr. F. Cress Welshing deduced), the result is the same: For the past 4,000 years, Caucasians have always worked to destroy Afrikans and their culture. Less Blacks forget, despite the xenophilic Afrikan weakness that allowed Indo-Europeans to fatally undermine Egyptian civilization politically, there were many Blacks (including the leaders) who fought relentlessly to prevent the physical overthrow of ancient Afrikan culture, e.g., Pharaoh Ahmose 1 (ca 1580-1558 b.c.e.) who initiated Dynasty 18, by chasing the Hyksos from Lower Egypt; Thothmes 3, the Napoleon of Antiquity; and Rameses 3 who fought five epic battles against Caucasian hordes, including one coalition of Whites that was the greatest witnessed in Antiquity.

If it is not obvious already to the reader, the ancient Egyptians were forced to enslave Caucasians to stem the unending invasions of their homeland. C.A. Diop (in Precolonial Black Africa) informs us that slaves of the

Egyptians were not comparable to the plebeian of ancient Rome, the thete of Athens, or the sudra (an "untouchable") of India. Ancient Egypt never developed a slave economy as did Greece and Rome; the Black psyche and law would not allow it. As a matter of fact, the freed descendants of White slaves were to pave the way for the conquest of Egypt in 661 b.c.e. by the white Assyrian Ashurbanipal.

Dr. Diop states that 661 b.c.e. marks the decline of Black political supremacy in Antiquity and in history; conscious, contemporary Afrika can attest to this tragic fact only too well. Even if uninspired by the cultural imperative to return and redevelop their original homeland (Africa), weak-minded U.S. Negroes might reconsider their sick attempts to identify with European-Americans given the disastrous effect of white psycho-social behavior upon the black people of ancient Egypt and Ethiopia.

Chapter 3

The Ancient Greek and Roman Experience: A Stolen Legacy

(To J.G. Jackson, Geo. G.M. James, and deGraft Johnson)

> Of all nations, those submit to civilization with the most difficulty who habitually live by the chase [i.e., nomads].[1] The heavy wagon with its wooden wheels ... was the nomad's house, ... Nomadic life of the IndoEuropeans is confirmed by the absence of any generic term denoting the word 'city' in the primitive foundation of the Indo-European vocabulary.[2] Lord Raglan rightly says, 'The Whites were, it seems, incapable of civilizing themselves . . . ("The Future of Civilization" in the <u>Rationalist Annual</u>, p. 40, 1946)'.[3]

> During al the nomadic period and for a long time after settlement in fixed abodes, the ideas of justice seemed unknown to the Aryans. Al their moral values were the opposite of those of the South cradle [Afrika] and were only to become milder on contact with this region [Afrika]. Crime violence, war, and a taste for risk, so many sentiments born of the [inclement, harsh] climate and the early conditions of [nomadic] existence, all predisposed the Aryan world [Europe], extraordinary as this may appear, to a great [infamous] historical destiny. The North cradle [Europe], confined to Greece and Rome, is characterized by the city-state. The particular character of these city-states, outside of which a man was an outlaw, developed an internal patriotism, as well as xenophobia [fear of strangers]. Individualism, moral and material

solitude, a disgust for existence, all the subject matter of modern literature, which even in its philosophic aspects is none other than the expression of the tragedy of a way of life [nomadism] going back to the Aryans' ancestors, are all attributes of this cradle [Europe]. An ideal of war, violence, crime, and conquests, inherited from nomadic life, is the special attribute of this cradle.

All historians and ethnologists who have compared African and Asian societies have been led to consider Western Asia as the land of lechery [corruption], in contrast to the healthiness of African customs.[4] ...' The whites have always been an unjust, jealous, unmerciful, avaricious, and blood-thirsty set of beings always seeking after power and authority--we view them all over the confederacy of Greece, ... we see them there, cutting each other's throats ...' (David Walker's Appeal, 1829).[5]

The preceding analyses reveal clearly the psychic characteristics of Caucasians, of ancient yesteryear and today, and the reasons for those mental traits. Thousands of years of isolation in a cold and barren environment (Europe), which necessitated a nomadic existence, resulted in the imbedding of specific values in Whites. Extreme individualism, xenophobia, acute materialism, avarice (greed), jealousy, thievishness, dishonesty, criminality, and violence (see the partial war-chronology of Europeans and White Asians in the Introduction to this text) are all traits resulting from the ancient and prolonged nomadic lifestyle of Indo-Europeans. It should not surprise the Black reader that the destructive psycho-social characteristics just described were transferred to the Caucasians' inhumane and highly exploitative economic system, i.e., ancient slavery, medieval feudalism (semi-slavery), and modern capitalism (neo-slavery). Even in uninspired by the cultural imperative to return and redevelop their original homeland (Afrika), weakminded U.S. Negroes given the disastrous effect of white psycho-social behavior upon the Black people of ancient Egypt and Ethiopia (see Chapter Two).

The purpose of this chapter is, in part, to examine the psycho-social condition of Caucasians and, specifically, the ancient Greeks. The ancient Greeks are acknowledged generally as the first civilized Indo-Europeans (Homer was the first literate White, ca 881 b.c.e.) and are heralded as the creators of Western civilization. To dispute that last allegation, the Black reader should acquire a copy of Dr. Y.A.A. ben-Jochannan's Africa: Mother of Western Civilization from his/her local Black bookstore. European cultural imperialism (domination) being what it is, perhaps the reader can recall having been taught that the ancient Greeks were even the originators of Western civilization. That is a distinct lie, as was revealed by the last chapter and as much of this present chapter will indicate.

[In ancient Europe] Public authority stopped at the door of a man's house.

> 'The time when man believed only in domestic gods is also the time when only families existed. Man cannot free himself easily of opinions which have once taken control of him.'

> Domestic worship separated individuals even to the grave, for even in after-life the families did not mix. For a long time this form of worship was supreme over others. In the beginning, the national divinities themselves were domestic, and belonged to private families. This private domestic character is a common feature of the Aryan and Semitic gods. Indeed, even after the triumph of monotheism in the human consciousness, Jehovah was to remain the god of his 'chosen people', as he was, in the beginning, the tribal god whom no

stranger could worship. There is no universal salvation: He only loves and saves his own.

> 'In death itself or in the existence which followed it, families did not mix with each other. The isolation of each property was so obligatory, that the two domains [tombs] could not border one on the other, and there had to be left between them a stretch of land which was neutral and which remained inviolate [untouched].'

Joint use, even between two households, was a sacrilege. On the formation of the [Aryan] cities, the law of isolation prevailed. Because of the religion, no other form of social organization than the city was possible. Each was sovereign, with its own system of weights and measures, its calendar, its feasts, and its records, and could not conceive of any overriding authority. The very nature of the institutions was opposed thus to the unification of the territories to form a [Aryan] nation.[6]

Even Plato [a famed Greek philosopher] in his Republic [a treatise on government], could not rise above the idea of a city-state.[7] Aryans, as long as they were relatively isolated in their northern cradle [Europe], never had the ability to conceive of a political, judicial, and social state of organization extending beyond the limits of the city.[8] Hostilities between those [Greek] villages even seemed childish: stones were thrown at inhabitants of a neighboring town as they passed through another community.[9] The notion of the state, of a 'territory' comprising several cities, or that of empire without question came to them [Aryans] from the southern world [Afrika], and in particular from the example of [ancient] Egypt. There could be no question of [Aryans] settling conquered populations on one's own territory and giving them residency, as MernePtah [20th Dynasty, ca 1232-1224 b.c.e.] and other Pharaohs of Egypt had done with Aryan peoples each time they conquered them. [Aryan] Families of different citizens constituting the city were separate cells, ..., these feelings of independence going back to life on the [Eurasian] steppes. But each [Aryan] individual, each family head, each citizen was directly riveted to the dictatorial state by a bond of bronze [i.e., a bronze sword].[10] The Greeks confined the admission to Paradise [Heaven] to the free-born.[11] Only the members of this class [eupatridea or patricians: ancient White hereditary aristocracy] could possess land in the sacred [religious] sense of the term. They alone, having ancestors, could have a domestic cult and a god, without which one had no political, judicial, or religious personality and was thus 'impure', a plebeian. Superstition and conservatism were inherent in them [the Greek eupatridae and Roman patricians]. This owning class alone was patriotic since only it had a 'patria,' i.e., freedom of the city, while the plebes [the multitudinous have-nots of ancient White society], without hearth [a sacred, religious fire] or home, were restricted to the low parts of the city, like the untouchables [i.e., the Sudra] of India. [12] As in all Indo-Aryan societies, Celtic [Irish] society had its lower orders composed of 'declasses' (especially those having lost at the winter games); of the dispossessed, expelled from the families to escape a blood debt or debt of money, etc.

These 'without hearth or house' were very numerous in Gaul [ancient France], according to Caesar.[13]

We have witnessed extreme individualism, which resulted from a prolonged nomadic existence, institutionalized in ancient Greco-Roman society in the form of religion and countless family gods.

Religious worship, as an expression of individualism, became the means by which White families separated themselves into unchangeable classes and the aristocracy (the 'haves') maintained an authority for control of the ponderous, lower class. Just as extreme, Indo-European individualism was reflected in religion, it become institutionalized in the form of an exploitative economic system, i.e. slavery, that relied predominantly upon grossly unequal class divisions; extreme individualism, resulting from a personal need to secure a material existence during 1,000s of years of nomadic life, helps to explain the slave economies of ancient Greece and Rome. The difficulty of securing an adequate material existence in barren, post-glacial Europe explains the capacity of Caucasians to build inhumane socio-economic systems beginning with slavery (and later medieval feudalism and modern capitalism) no matter what atrocities are committed upon others (the vast majority of slaves in Antiquity were White).

Can the Black reader detect a similarity between the 'impure' underclass of Greek thetes and Roman plebeians and untouchable East Indian Sudras confined to the undesirable parts of ancient Aryan cities and the numerous, present-day individuals confined to the so-called ghetto parts of cities in European-America? As a product of thousands of years of barbaric, nomadic life and the desperation of each Aryan to secure food, shelter, and clothing in inclement Europe, extreme individualism fostered acute materialism and xenophobia (the fear of strangers). Given the xenophobic, White mentality extending from prehistory, integration-mad Negroes in America might do well to understand that it has not been the historical nature of Caucasians to settle (integrate) conquered populations within Caucasian society. I shall present next another product of White individualism, patriarchy, which ensures that social and material rights are transmitted through males; patriarchy (or patrilineal succession) has allowed for the domination of females by males.

> F. de Coulanges [in La Cite Antique, 1930]
> showed that individual right among Aryans was
> anterior to the foundation of cities, and that this is
> the reason why, for a long time, the state had no
> power to interfere in the private life of families,
> that is to say that in Rome and Greece during

whole centuries a man could kill his son, his wife, or his slaves, or sell them, without committing a crime against the state, which was then the city. As far as we can go back into the Indo-European past, even so far back as the Eurasian steppes, there is only to be found the patrilineal genos [clan].[14]

A main theme of the Greek myth is the gradual reduction of women from sacred beings to chattel. The Greeks adopted Hesoid's fable of Pandora's [the female who unleashed the evils of the world upon mankind] jar.[15] According to Caesar, in Gaul, Rome, and Ireland, the paternal head had the right of life and death over his children and wife. This practice [the abandonment of children and the burial of infant girls] remained customary among the Greeks even after their settling down, and they were stupefied to see the Egyptians raise all their children without distinction of sex, instead of abandoning an appreciable number at birth, as so much rubbish.

Polyandry is the exclusive property of the Indo-Aryans, with the exception of the Semites. It consists of forcing a woman, against her will, to assure the descent of a group of brothers or others. We have seen it to flourish in Athens [Greece], as here in an Anglo-Saxon country [ancient Ireland]. H. Hubert [in Les Celtes, 1950] explains Celtic [Irish] polyandry by the economic inferiority of the woman in the social system: from a material point of view, the men were interested in introducing as few women as possible into the group.

In Europe, during the classical [ancient] age, (Greece, Rome), ... no accident could lead a women to reign. She occupied a position similar to that of a slave, to the extent that, having no

> juridical individuality she was unable to serve as a witness, was cloistered [secluded] in the gynaeceum [women's apartments], was unable to take part in any public deliberation, her husband had the right of life and death over her, and had the right to sell her and her children, with whom he could also abandon. However, the 'prostitutes' were the only women who enjoyed the esteem and the consideration of the intellectual elite, ...[16]

The Black female reader should compare the subhuman condition of ancient White females with the health and privileged condition of Afrikan women in Egypt and Ethiopia (see Chapter Two); Black women should seek Dr. C.A. Diop's The Cultural Unity of Black Africa for an extensive analysis of the completely opposite positions of females in Aryan and Afrikan cultures, respectively. From prehistorical (pre 3200 and 4236 b.c.e. times until today, the patrilineal transference of socio-political rights has insured maledominated Western (and Arab and E. Indian, etc.) societies. Black women in the U.S. might scrutinize their Caucasianized Negro male counterparts closely; since EuropeanAmerican cultural domination has wiped Negro memories clean of their prior Afrikan culture (including matriarchy), Black women can expect Negro males to adopt increasingly the European male's mentality toward females. That thought should curdle the blood of a historically conscious Black woman.

The same European-American cultural imperialism, in the form of White scholarship, that has erased the contemporary Negro's memory of Afrikan tradition would have Blacks think that the first creators of civilization were White and civilization originated in one of three societies, respectively, i.e., Sumer(ia), Crete (see The 1987 Information Please Almanac, p. 106), or Greece. Despite current Negrophobia, the original inhabitants of both Sumer and Crete were Black. The remainder of this chapter will help to dispel Negrophobic insinuations that Greeks were the originators of civilization.

> The reigns of Cecrops, a legendary king of Egyptian origin, is generally situated at this same period of the Pelasgians [proto-Greeks]. It is he

who is said to have introduced into Greece the practices of the South [Afrika]-agriculture--and even, it seems, the custom of marriage. In Greece, tradition says that it is to Cecrops and Egyptos, both sons of Egypt, that one must go back for the adoption of agriculture as a national activity.

'The history of the Greek countries begins in these XVIth to XVth centuries before our era [i.e., 1500-1400 b.c.e.].... The seals [on documents] of [Egyptian Pharaoh] Amenophis III and his queen Tii (1411-1380 b.c.) found in Cyprus, Rhodes, Crete, and Mycena, furnish the first certain date for the full advancement of this Aegaeo-Levantine civilization [Greece], ...'[17]

By conservative estimates, the ancient Egyptians had been recording their history for 1,700 years before they taught the Greeks the elements of civilization. Lo and behold, even according to Greek tradition (mythology), the ancestors of Niggers in America are the very ones responsible for teaching the nomadic Greeks the art of agriculture. Greek tradition states further that Egyptians (the ancestors of present-day so-called Niggers in the U.S.) taught the barbaric Greeks the alphabet, written laws, metallurgy, and how to build the fleet, 50-oared "Homeric" vessel. Concerning the so-called Homeric vessel created by Egyptians, the Black reader can appreciate the following tragic irony: In ca 202 b.c.e., after 60 years of battle, the Romans utilized the Homeric vessel to destroy the last great North Afrikan (Black) civilization along the southern Mediterranean Sea; the annihilation of Carthage, founded originally in 822 b.c.e. by migrating Phoenician Blacks, marks the point after which Caucasians penetrated unceasingly and destroyed all of Afrika eventually. It must be said in passing that the Blacks did not allow the razing (burning) of their homeland without fighting for every square inch of Carthage; i.e., Carthagian Blacks fought the Romans from street to street and from house to house.

According to the Black mental-giant Dr. George G.M. James (in his seminal work, <u>Stolen Legacy</u>), the Greeks copied the name of their maritime (sea) god Proteus from the Egyptian Pharaoh

Proteus of Dynasty 18 or 19; the Greeks showed their admiration for the world's original civilization by copying other Nile Valley gods including Osiris (the original Christ) whom they renamed Dionysus (the disguised hero of all Greek tragic theatre according to F.W. Nietzsche, a famed German philosopher). Historians inform us that Solon, a Greek legislator, showed his great regard for ancient Black high-culture by traveling to study the Egyptian government before drafting laws for his own homeland. Indeed, as I shall report, the well-reknown philosopher Pythagoras and a host of Greek scientists copied, stole, and plagiarized more Egyptian knowledge than can be recounted.

> ... Ideas attributed to Pythagoras are without any doubt of Egyptian origin. That is why an Egyptian priest told Diodorus of Sicily that once the Greeks returned home, they took credit for all the sciences they learned in Egypt.[18] The Egyptian priests did not put their names to their discoveries as did the individualistic Greeks, and no inventor's name has survived. On the contrary, they kept them jealously within the bosom of their caste and only dispensed an exoteric [superficial] elementary teaching to the people. We know today in an almost certain fashion that Thales of Miletus, Pythagoras of Samos, Archimedes of Sicily, Plato, Solon, etc. had been pupils of the Egyptian priests, who at this period, even according to Plato, considered the Greeks as relatively childish [immature, unsophisticated] minds. Such a taste for the individual reputation of the immortality of the name, such a lack of intellectual honestly, did not fail to anger the honest Herodotus, who showed, without beating about the bush, that Pythagoras was a plagiarist (cf. Herodotus, Book II).[19] The Rhind papyrus shows that the Egyptians did invent arithmetic and geometric progressions. All the operations that Pythagoras made--summations in particular--were commonly made by the Egyptians.[20]

The [eternal] salvation (of the soul) was the reward which the Pythagorean philosophical system offered its initiates.[21] And it is seen that it is not only due to chance that among the Negroes of Black Africa and the ancient Egyptians, who all practised totemism or zoolatry (both of which make possible the identification of a human being and an animal), that vitalism was at the basis of their conception of the universe. In a mentality where the essence of things, ontology par excellence, is the vital force, the exterior forms of beings and of objects become secondary. This unrestrained worship of animals, this zoolatry, which the Greeks jeered at so much, and of which A. Aymard remarks that no traces were to be found in Semitic [Jewish or Arabic] Asia. It is within the framework of such [Afrikan] thought, that were logically situated the philosophical doctrines such as that of the reincarnation or metempsychosis of Pythagoras. Herodotus, in paragraph 124 of his second book takes up ironically the attribution of this doctrine [i.e., transmigration of the soul] to Pythagoras. He [Herodotus] says there that he knows someone [Pythagoras] in Greece who, wishing to give himself a reputation as scholar and philosopher attributed to himself this doctrine which was invented by Egyptians, but who, by discretion, he does not wish to name.[22]

The 'Doctrine of Opposites' attributed to Pythagoras [and Heraclitus] originated in the [Egyptian] Mysteries [Educational] System as demonstrated by the pairs of gods representing positive and negative principles of nature.[23]

Albert Slosman writes: 'For let us not forget that it was because of rampant use of plagiarism among the Greeks that Clement of Alexandria said at the time: "A one thousand [1,000] page book will not be long enough to cite the names of my fellow countrymen who have used and abused Egyptian science.'" Hippocrates [the Greek and Western father of medicine] had consulted the annals [records] of Imhotep [the Egyptian multi-genius architect-physician of the 3rd Dynasty, ca 2780 b.c.e.] in the Memphis temple Library in the fifth century [b.c.e.]. The influence of Egyptian medicine on Greek medicine can be observed. For example, the method given in the Carlsberg papyrus no. 4, whether it is true or false, has been copied out verbatim by the [so-called] 'father of medicine' [Hippocrates]: I refer to the clove of garlic method for diagnosing sterility in women.[24] The Encyclopedia Britannica says, ... 'His [Imhotep's] prestige increased with the lapse of centuries and his temples in Greek times were the centres of medical teaching. '[25]

As early as the fourth millennium [3,000s] b.c., the Egyptians had already created leap year. We have seen that the two Egyptian calendars were already in use during the first dynasty [3200-2980 b.c.e.]. This did not prevent Diagenes Laerces, the Thales' biographer (6th century [500s] b.e.), from writing that he was the first to divide the year into 365 days. In his treatise entitled 'On the Equilibrium of Planes or Centres of Gravity in Planes,' nowhere did Archimedes show that the Egyptians had already mastered the theory of levers of all kinds, as well as that of the inclined plane, before he did. Like all Greek scientists, Archimedes went to study or to further his studies in Egypt.[26]

All the mechanical inventions attributed to Archimedes present a doubtful character; they existed in Egypt 1,000s of years before the birth of

Archimedes. The builders of the pyramids of the ancient [Egyptian] empire knew the principle of the lever; they employed the latter, in a variety of ways, to hoist tons of rock to the tops of the pyramids under construction. Now it is impossible to use such an instrument without immediately recognizing the relationship between mass and distance, without theorizing. Archimedes is said to have discovered the endless screw, which is at the origin of enormous mechanical progress. But Diodorus Siculus is quite definite Archimedes could only have made this invention after his voyage to Egypt, where the hydraulic screw was already in use and served to pump water. This appears so obvious that it is readily accepted today that Archimedes had at the most adapted an Egyptian invention. Finally, even the Principle of Archimedes deals with this mechanics of fluids. There are, therefore, grounds for pursuing the investigations. The outcome would seem to be obvious.[27]

In their arithmetic, the Greeks have kept the old Egyptian fraction notation [derived during the Old Kingdom] of 2200 b.c. It must be said that, traditionally, philosophers and scientists were persecuted [e.g., Socrates] in the Greek-Anthenian state. ... It is important to remember that the formula $C = (pi)D$ is attributed to Dinostratus. This formula which gives the length of the circumference is believed to have been established by the Egyptians 1,400 years before its alleged Greek author.[28] The Theorem of Thales concerns similar triangles. This theory was part of the Rhind papyrus, which is in the British museum. It (problem 53 of the Rhind papyrus) represents the Thales Theorem 1,300 years before his birth. And we have nothing written by him that he wrote this Theorem which is attributed to him. When the

Egyptians arrived at this mathematics, the Greeks did not exist yet, as a people, in history.[29] V. Struve concludes that it therefore stands to reason that the Greeks explicitly admitted that Egyptians were their masters in the field of geometry which came to Greece from Egypt and not from Babylonia. Struve also insists on the accuracy of Egyptian geometry.[30]

It is shown that the Greeks--Pythagoras, Hippocrates, Diagenes, Laerces, Archimedes, Dinostratus, and Thales--stole or are attributed with medical, mathematical, and mechanical inventions that are the product of Egyptian civilization; ancient documents affirm this. Of course, the reader has been warned of the Caucasian's Northeast Afrika syndrome--that is, an effort to whiten the Black creators of civilization--in the absence of being able to assign the elements of the first civilization to the Greeks (Whites). The following remarks by Sir E.A.W. Budge, one of Britain's two greatest Egyptologists, are a specific example of the White man's North-east Afrika syndrome. "About the race to which the Egyptian known to us from mummies and statues belongs and his characteristics, there is no doubt whatever. He was a Caucasian, and it would seem that he came to Egypt from an original home in Asia [The Mummy, pp. 1-2]." Budge's declarations are an outright lie, as has been shown already in Chapter Two.

Of the Greek scientists mentioned above, Pythagoras might rank supreme as an intellectual thief who claimed knowledge which he knew had originated with the ancient Egyptians; even modern-day high school graduates can recall the mathematical theorems concerning triangles to which Pythagoras' name is attached. There are now two points upon which the Black reader must focus seriously. Utilizing C.A. Diop's Two Cradle theory, I have stated earlier in this chapter that a temperament of greed, thievishness, and dishonesty in Caucasians is due to 1,000s of years of isolation in cold and barren Europe which resulted in a cruel, nomadic existence. In this light, the thievish acts of ancient Greek scientists can be understood as a psychological reflex to secure their material existence by dishonestly building their reputations. I insist that the thievish and dishonest traits exhibited by the early

Greek scientists and thinkers are the exact same psycho-social characteristics of Aryans today (e.g., witness the Whites' occupation of the stolen Indian empire of No. America). Throughout this text, I have advocated that historicallyconscious and technologically-prepared Blacks in the U.S. plan to return to their original homeland in order to assist Afrika reclaim her rightful political and industrial position in the world; certainly only an unconscious Negro would suggest that Blacks continue to languish (not bask!) in the sunshine of European-American society. If the premise that the psycho-social traits of Aryans are antithetical (completely opposite) to those of Afrikans is accepted, then the reader will understand that Caucasians have never lived in any society with Blacks without seeking to control and dominate them; if they were alive today, it is obvious the ancient Blacks of Egypt, Ethiopia, Phoenicia (Canaan), and Carthage, whose high-cultures were destroyed by Caucasians, would agree with my premise? As I shall illustrate in the remaining chapters, the great empires of medieval and modern Afrika would be destroyed also, in turn, by Caucasians.

A second point must be focused upon. The reader should understand that White cultural imperialism--in the form of academic Negrophobia, for example--is intended to insure the psychological and economic domination of Blacks. By coopting (stealing) the achievements of Afrikan civilizations, European-American mis-scholarship diminishes the worth and stature of Blacks in the minds of the public and prepares the way for the mental and physical annihilation (genocide) of Black people.

To V. Berard [<u>The Resurrection of Homer. The Heroic Age</u>.], the
Egypto-
Phoenicians played the same civilizing role
towards Greece and the Hebrews, if not more so,
as did Greco-Latin antiquity towards the modern
West.

> The error of our predecessors was only in
> believing that the dawn of modern times was
> also the awakening of creative and thinking
> humanity, and that Homer [the first literate
> White, ca 881 b.c.e.] and the Bible were the

first sudden explosions of literary genius. The recent discoveries of the archaeologists in Egypt and Chaldea [according to Diodorus of Sicily, a colony of Black astrologer-priests who lived along the Euphrates River, but who were formerly from Egypt] have fully revealed to us that during a long Levantine [East Mediterranean] antiquity, scholars, artists, and poets had already created masterpieces, which were also to serve as models for a hundred [100] generations and of which Hebrews and Hellens [Greeks], far from being ignorant of these, where the admirers and imitators and sometimes even the copyists.[31]

Without any doubt, these universalist ideas [of Anexagoras, the Sophists (Greek philosophers), and Zeno, etc.] derived from the southern world and in particular from Egypt. These conceptions [e.g., the idea of a universal God] which Christianity later adopted were not originally a part of it [Christianity], it seems.[32] F. de Coulanges [in La Cite Antique] insists that, for a considerable length of time, the idea of a universal god never touched Greco-Roman thought.

'It must be recognized that the ancients, excepting certain rare superior intellects, never represented God as a unique being exercising power over the whole universe. As to the God of the human type, some philosophers were able to guess at it, the mysteries of Eleusis [i.e., the mysteries of Dionysus] made it possible to glimpse at it for the most intelligent of their initiates, but the mass of the people never believed in it. for a long time man only understood the divine being as a force which protected him personally, and each man or group of men wished to have his own [domestic] gods.'

F. de Coulanges counted the number of gods there were in Rome: they were more numerous than the citizens: 'there are in Rome more gods than citizens.'[33]

Memphite [Egyptian] Theology is the source of Greek philosophy or primitive science and is the basis of modern scientific [heliocentric] belief.[34] Most of the scientists [or philosophers] who gave Greece its scientific fame were persecuted and had to flee from Greece to take refuge in Egypt. Almost all of them went to Egypt for training. Anexagoras, Socrates, Aristotle, and Plato were persecuted or had to flee to escape persecution.[35] [The Doctrine of Mind according to Anexagoras:] The mind alone is self-moved and is the cause [creator] of all motion in the universe and has the supreme power over all things. The Doctrine of Mind attributed to Socrates [and Anexagoras]-- 'Whatsoever exists for a useful purpose is the work of an Intelligence'--is represented by the [Egyptian] god Osiris' all-seeing Eye.

[Plato's 'Theory of Ideas':] The Idea [concept, noumen] is real; but the thing [phenomena] known by the concept is unreal and imperfect. Plato's 'Theory of Ideas' is based upon the 'Doctrine of Opposites' which was stolen by Pythagoras from the Egyptian Mysteries System. 'Timaeus' is the title of Plato's plagiarized work and the name, according to Josephus [an ancient Jewish historian], of a Dynasty 15 Egyptian pharaoh. In his Doctrine of Transmigration, Plato copied the Judgment Scene of the ancient Egyptian Book of the Dead. Both Plato and Aristotle copied the [Egyptian] god Atum and stole the concept of the demiurge or Uncreated Creator from the Memphis Theology of ancient Egypt.

To prove the existence of God, Aristotle used the Doctrine of Teleology:

> The purpose and design in nature is the work of [Divine] Intelligence.
> Aristotle stole the concept of the Uncreated Creator and copied the Memphite [Egyptian] god Atum who sat unmoved [uncreated] on the Primeval Hill [at the origin of the world].[36]

Through the testimony of ancient eyewitness Herodotus, it is confirmed that the master intellectual-thief Pythagoras stole the following spiritual or philosophical concepts from the Egyptians: transmigration (the departure of the soul from the body); immortality of the soul; and eternal salvation. Thanks to George G.M. James' incomparable work Stolen Legacy, to which one must refer in order to explicate (explain) the above passages, the reader can add the names of Anexagoras, Plato, and Aristotle to that endless list of individualistic Greek thinkers who plagiarized or stole the knowledge of the ancient Europeans. As an uncivilized and barbaric bunch, Indo-Europeans were obliged to travel to Egypt, the source of knowledge in Antiquity, in somewhat the same fashion as presentday Blacks--whose prior civilizations have been destroyed--are required to study at European institutions. Tragically for Blacks, the philosopher-thief Aristotle stole countless Egyptian books from the temples of Memphis (present-day Cairo) in 332 b.c.e. while he accompanied the armies of Alexander the Great during the conquest and rape of Egypt. In passing, it must be added that as militarily great as Alexander was, his invasion of Afrika was stopped by Ethiopian Queen Candace who stood in front of her troops at the Nubian border (see C. Williams, The Destruction of Black Civilization, p. 125).

Even given the long and cruel nomadic existence of Aryans, is the Black reader able to appreciate the ingratitude of the war-minded Greeks of 332 b.c.e. who subjugated (conquered) the very people (Egyptians) who had taught them the art of civilization hundreds of years earlier? A close scrutiny of the destructive acts of ancient Greeks against Egypt, the mother of civilization, will provide crucial insight into the warlike and destructive mentality of modern-day Caucasians.

> In Egypt, the seven Liberal Arts [i.e., the Quadrivium and Trivium] were intended to

liberate [free] the soul [mind] from its ten bodily [i.e., physical, sensual] fetters.[37]

Charlemagne was crowned in the year 800 a.d. He [Charlemagne--a king of
Frankish people who inhabited the territory which became modern-day France] created the Holy Roman Empire. His tutor Alcuin played a key role in unearthing and diffusing the knowledge of antiquity, especially through commentary on the works of Aristotle. The transmission to modern man of the Trivium (dialectics, rhetoric, grammar) and the Quadrivium (arithmetic, geometry, astronomy, music) was thus assured [in Europe]. As the Turks occupied Constantinople destroying the Eastern [Roman] Empire, Greek scholars fled to the West [i.e., Europe]. The intellectual influence of Aristotle, the only Greek philosopher to be studied, was considerable on the thinkers of the Middle Ages. His [Aristotle's] authority was almost sacrosanct [holy]: thanks to him, they [Europeans] little by little familiarized themselves with the rational, scientific manner of thinking.

> 'Led by Plato, ... [ancient Athens in Greece] shone with the seven liberal arts .... At the end of the twelfth century, Paris [France] would seem the new Athens'.

Through the Arab philosophers Avicenna and Averroes, Aristotle become known and discussed in the West [beginning specifically in Spain, ca 711
c.e.]. It was the Arabs who introduced the Aristotelian texts to Europe, well before the Crusaders [i.e., European Christians] contact [in ca 1096 c.e.] with Byzantium [Western Asia]. They [the Arabs] introduced the same texts into Black Africa in the same period.

> The Trivium, i.e., the study of grammar, Aristotelian logic (formal logic, grammatical logic), and rhetoric, was on the list of subjects taught [in medieval West Afrika], as shown in the <u>Tarikh es Sudan</u>. The intellectual tradition was already well established at the time of Sadi [the Black Islamic scholar of the 1500s c.e. who wrote the <u>Tarikh es Sudan</u>.[38]

The first three chapters of this text should have given the reader some insight into the marvelous and endless number of philosophical and scientific achievements of ancient Afrikan high-cultures: In antiquity, Blacks created all the theosophical and technological elements of civilization which they proceeded generously to disseminate (transmit) to the entire world. While Egypt (or Egypto-Ethiopia) had been the cradle of civilization for 10,000 years (see C.A. Diop, <u>The African Origin of Civilization</u>, p. 10), it must be remembered that Egyptian high-culture was destabilized and began to crumble rapidly beginning with the invasion of armies of the White Assyrian Ashurbanipal in 661 b.c.e.; after this point, castes of Egyptian (Kemite) priests, who had zealously guarded the theosophical and technical knowledge, fled their homeland. Consequently, Afrika was to lose its command of the theoretical, physical sciences (i.e., high mathematics, physics, etc.). It should bring tears to the eyes of the Black reader to consider how politically and technologically developed the Afrikan continent would be if not for the unending series of Caucasian invasions beginning in Antiquity and continuing through the modern era.

Ancient Nile Valley Afrikans discovered all the elements of civilization including the seven liberal arts (i.e., the trivium and quadrivium). Tragic irony, in Afrikan and World history, is revealed in the person of the philosopher-thief Aristotle, who stole texts from the temples of Memphis, Egypt (the Greeks renamed Memphis into Alexandria) and whose works have been crammed down the throats of contemporary U.S. Blacks in the form of Euro-American studies; one can deduce from the prior references that the study of philosopher-thief Aristotle's works among the Europeans led to their Renaissance (ca 1400-1700 c.e.), etc. In the preceding quoted passages, it should trouble greatly the Black reader to see the White Arabs, of the 11th century c.e., teaching West Afrikans the very academic disciplines the Afrikans themselves created 1,000s of years earlier. The knowledge of the humanities and sciences, which the Egyptians had developed (as late as Dynasty 4, ca 2565 b.c.e.) and later taught the Greeks from 1400-30 b.c.e., was recopied by the Arabs and preserved during the European Dark Ages (ca 700-1100 c.e.); this technical knowledge, created by the ancient Egyptians and cultivated by Greeks, was to become the foundation of the mechanical science which fueled the European Industrial Revolution (ca 1730-1850 c.e.) of the modern era.[39]

Chapter 4

Afrikan Origins of Religious Thought and the Major Western Religions:
Judaism, Christianity and Islam

(To my psychological mentor, ben-Jochannan)

They [religious ideas] are illusions, fulfillments of the oldest, strongest and most urgent wishes of mankind.[1] Man created God to answer our fear of the unknown which we call - Nether World, Heaven, and even the Hereafter (including 'hell' etc.)[2] In ancient times, the multitudes could only be led to religion and virtue through superstition, prodigies [the supernatural], and fables.[3]

The advance of thought tends to strip the old animal and plant [totemic] gods of their bestial and vegetable husk, and to leave their human attributes (which are always the kernel of the conception) as the final and sole residuum. When plant and animal [totemic] gods have become wholly or nearly anthropomorphic [humanized], the animals and plants which were at first deities themselves, still retain a vague and ill-understood connection with the anthropomorphic gods who have developed out of them.[4] It is in fact natural for man to personify [i.e., to assign human qualities to; humanize] everything that he wants to understand in order later to control it...[5] Primitives believe that the world [the forces of nature, etc.] is operated by supernatural beings with impulses and emotions like themselves. Man in fact created gods in his own likeness [i.e., anthropomorphism] and being himself mortal, he naturally supposed his creatures [gods] to be in the same sad predicament.[6]

In the course of time, the first observations were made of the regularity and conformity to law in natural phenomena, and with this the forces of nature lost their human traits. But man's helplessness [against the forces of nature] remains and along with it his [psychological] longing for his father [who protected him during his childhood helplessness], and the gods [to protect him against the ills of society and the forces of nature]. Thus man's longing for a father [protector] is a motive identical with his need for protection against the consequences of his human weakness. Defense against childish helplessness is what lends its characteristic features to the adult's reaction to the helplessness which he has to acknowledge--a [psychological; physical] reaction which is precisely the formation of religion. And thus a store of ideas is created, born from man's need to make his helplessness tolerable... [for example:] Everything that happens in this world is an expression of the intentions of an intelligence superior to us, ... It now became the task of the gods to even out the defects and evils of civilization.

And thus a store of ideas is created, born from man's need to make his helplessness tolerable... [for example:] Life after death ... brings people all the perfection that one may perhaps have missed here.[7]

I have assumed innocently that the well-renown, White anthropologist Sir J.G. Frazier would have considered the primeval plant and animal gods referred to above as totemic in nature; a totem is a plant or animal species from which a clan or group of people claim descent. However, the Black historian J.G. Jackson (<u>An Introduction to African Civilizations</u>, pp. 52-3) states explicitly that a totem is not a god and that totemism is not the worship of plants or animals as gods; it can be interpreted that totemism was the world's first theory of evolution and was utilized by primeval matrilineal and agricultural societies in Afrika to regulate the efficient and equitable production and distribution of food.

It is necessary for the Black reader to differentiate between totemism and the distorted, European perception that Afrikans have worshipped animal or plant gods. Totemism is a significant topic for Black discussion since it involves also the concepts of metaphysical vitalism (i.e., the idea that the psychological or spiritual force/essence of one being can be transferred to another being) and ontology {i.e., the origin and nature of being and matter). It is crucial for the black reader to discern (understand) that totemism and monotheism (the concept of one god) and the xenophilic vulnerability of Afrikans can be traced to their innate vitalistic and ontological concepts that all life (including plants and animals) is part of one universal essence; one should remember from Chapter Two that the trait of xenophilia (peaceful, loving) among Blacks allowed the Egyptians to accept Caucasians into that ancient Nile Valley high-culture which paved the way for its destruction. Historically speaking, the tradition of metaphysical vitalism and totemism which provides that all animals (including humans) and plants originate from one essence has been missing from White people (see C.A. Diop, The African Origin of Civilization, pp. 134-35); from that perspective, the acutely individualistic, xenophobic, and destructive Aryan characteristics may be better understood (but not better appreciated by Blacks!) and may provide again a basis for the analysis of the completely opposite European and Afrikan cultures, respectively.

A Diopian perspective on the origin of religion is that ancestor worship among ancient Afrikans formed the basis for their understanding of the origin of the world (The Afrikan Origin of Civilization, p. 140); likewise, ancestral worship formed the basis of religion among Caucasians (see Diop, The Cultural Unity of Black Afrika, p. 156; also, J.M. Robertson, Pagan Christs, pp. 14-15).

Ancestral worship among the ancient, individualistic Caucasians developed into countless domestic or family gods, as the reader witnessed in Chapter Three; on the contrary, ancestral worship among Afrikans evolved into monotheism (the concept and belief of one universal god).

> With the aid of the mildness of their physical surroundings, the Nubians [ancient Ethiopians] and the Egyptians had, at an early date, more than one thousand [1,000] years before the Greco-Latins [Greeks and Romans] and the Semites [Jews and Arabs], the idea of an all-powerful God, creator of all living things, benefactor of all humanity without distinction, and of whom anyone could become a disciple and gain salvation. Such a god was Ammon who, until the present day, is the God of the whole of West Africa: he is the one described by M. Griaule in his [book] <u>Dieu d'Eau</u> (God of Water); Amma, God of the Dogons, is indeed the god of water, of humidity, of fertility. He has the same attributes as Ammon, in the Sudan as well as in Nigeria among the Yoruba. Plutarch [an ancient Greek author], in <u>Isis and Osiris</u> thinks that the name [Ammon] signifies in Egyptian, 'hidden', 'invisible'.[8]

> There must have been vigorous intellectual movement in the late Old [Egyptian] Kingdom [ca 3200-2150 b.c.e.] when all the rest of the world ... was still engulfed in illiterate barbarism. By [ca 2565 b.c.e.] Dynasty 4 of the Old Kingdom, the intellectual pattern of Egyptian civilization was complete. The Egyptian priests and scribes were dealing with insoluble theological problems [both metaphysical and spiritual] two thousand [2,000] years before Christianity.

> The subtler Egyptian texts of Dynasties 1-9 are really about the nature of the human soul and the nature of God [Dynasties 1-10 represent the Old Kingdom]. Coffin Texts [of Dynasty 7] glosses [i.e., explanations entered in the margin of texts by

priests and scribes] show that some Egyptians were aware that really there was only one God....⁹ In Kemet [ancient Egyptian] mythology, the essence of God [Ptah] is revealed as thought (will) and command (intent).¹⁰

'... God is from the beginning, and He hath been from the beginning. He hath existed from of old and was when nothing else had being.... (E.A.W. Budge, <u>Egyptian Ideas of the Future</u>, p. 20)' The above is a description of the Egyptian Supreme Being,.... The Supreme Being for the Egyptians was without description.¹¹ The Pyramid Texts [of Dynasty 6] contain the oldest references to cosmogony [a theory of the creation of the universe] in terms of Atum [God]. This is still clearer from Utterance 587 [of the Pyramid Texts] which beings:

> 'Hail to you, O Atum!
> Hail to you, O Becoming One who came into being of himself [i.e., the Uncreated Creator]!'

Thus, in <u>Coffin Text 714</u> the High God says:

> 'I created my limbs in my 'glory.'
> I was maker of myself, in that I formed myself according to my desire and in accord with my heart.'¹²

During the Old, Middle, and New Kingdoms of ancient Egyptian history, various groups of priests referred to a supreme being by different names: Ra, Atum, Am(m)on, or Aton. It is clear absolutely, that Egyptians conceived of an all-powerful (omnipotent, omniscient), universal, supreme being. It is obvious that the ages-old, monotheistic principle among Afrikans remains strong even today since Amon (God), who came to prominence beginning in the pre-dynastic Saharan civilization (pre 7,000 b.c.e.) and who re-emerged during the Egyptian Middle Kingdom (ca 2100 b.c.e.), is still the supreme being among the traditional West Afrikans such as the Dogons of Mali, the Yoruba of Nigeria, etc. (see also C.A. Diop, The African Origin of Civilization, p. 66).

As the following passages will indicate, World history remembers Pharaoh Amenhotep 4 of Dynasty 18 as the individual who attempted to enforce the monotheistic concept, in the name of Aton, upon all ancient Egyptian priests at the same time.

> We [Blacks] must go back into our past and look for the origin of the theory about 'monotheism' which certain Jewish [Hebrew] scribes who wrote the Pentateuch (i.e., the Old Testament or Five Books of Moses, written ca. 700
>
> b.c.e.) attributed to... 'Moses' (b. 1320 b.c.e.) instead of its true African authority--Pharaoh Amenhotep 4th (1405-1370 b.c.e.), who was also known as 'Akhenaten, Ikhnaton, [Amenophis 4th]' etc.[13] It is Pharaoh Akhnaten who created the monotheistic religion. Akhnaten was the first to say that God is a spirit and was not created and should not be represented by images.
> It is the purest monotheism represented in religious history.[14] J. Breasted (in The Conquest of Civilization, 1926) considers Pharaoh Akhnaten as the first inventor of the purest form of monotheism in the history of humanity. The God Aton conceived by him was not distinguishable by any form of statutory representation; the solar disc symbolized his [Aton's] power, and by its brightness and its rays gave fresh life to all nature.[15]
>
> It is generally agreed that Akhnaten ('It is well with Aten') was the first to achieve the idea of monotheism. Atenism was a solar doctrine transformed by the substitution of abstractions and universals for gross details and local human myths. Aten was the single divine being who had created all things. Where Aten differed from Ra [God] was in his jealousy of other gods, his abhorrence of

sacred images of any kind, and the forthright condemnation of all other forms of worship.[16] The revolutionary concept of an eternal, omnipotent and only God was first proposed by Akhenaten and was either adopted or reinvented [?] by the Hebrews [Jews].[17] The doctrine of monotheism was not actualized in the body of the [Jewish] Old Testament until long after the Exile [or Jewish captivity by Nebuchadrezzar of Babylon which lasted until ca 538 b.c.e.], and perhaps as late as 300 b.c.[18]

The Egyptian name of Moses [Moshe] was given to all [Egyptian]
Mysteries [Educational] System initiates; it meant 'saved by water.'[19] Moses was, by tradition, learned in the wisdom of the Egyptians, and the Egyptian influence in early Israelite [Jewish, Hebrew] thought is evident in many places. Egyptologists have emphasized its [the name Moses] affinity to the Egyptian word mose, meaning son, while Yahuda equates it with the Egyptian mu-sheh, meaning 'child of the Nile.' Like Horus, the beloved god of Egypt, ..., Moses had been born in secret and hidden in a basket among bulrushes. A malicious god, Set, sought to destroy Horus; a malicious Pharaoh sought to destroy Moses. Buto, goddess of the north, found and reared Horus [the Egyptian Christ] while his mother visited him secretly; a Pharaoh's daughter found and reared Moses, his mother being employed as his nurse. When Horus grew to manhood he slew Set, who had wronged his father; when Moses grew to manhood, he slew an Egyptian who was wronging a Hebrew.[20]

I have covered tens of 1,000s of history in this chapter in an effort to examine, if not explain, the Afrikan origin of religions and some peculiarities of the major Western religions: Judaism,

Christianity, and Islam. The reader might ask why an examination of the origins of Judaism, Christianity, and Islam is necessary. Blacks in the U.S. (and around the world) have suffered military imperialism in the form of the Slave Trade and colonialism; consequently, Blacks are presently dominated by White economic and cultural (e.g., education, religion, etc.) institutions. Caucasian (and Negro) educational and religious institutions are responsible for Europeanizing the Black ming; the product of this process of Europeanization is integration-mad Negroes who refuse to develop an Afrikan historical consciousness or personality. If the Black reader has not understood already from this text that respective Afrikan and European cultures are irreconcilable, then I suggest that he/she not read further.

I have reason to pause momentarily since this chapter attempts to cover tens of 1,000s of years of history to discover the origin of religions. Whether or not the practice of totemism represents an initial stage of Afrikan ancestral worship which became religion, it helped nevertheless to shape the world's most perfect social organization as experienced in ancient Egypt and the rest of Afrika. The Black reader should recall from Chapter Three that, despite the urgings of White mis-scholarship, the Greek Pythagoras was not the originator of the principles of transmigration, immortality of the soul, and salvation; instead, it was the Afrikan concept of totemism (or so-called zoolatry) which led to the creation of the aforementioned metaphysical principles. Conceptually speaking, it seems that a corollary principle of totemism--metaphysical vitalism--provided an ontological (metaphysical) basis for the development of monotheism by Egyptian priests and Pharaoh Akhenaton.

I marvel at the continued success of White cultural imperialism; that is why, throughout this text, I have attacked Negrophobia as disseminated (spread) by White misscholarship. What psychological force could encourage Negroes (i.e., Caucasianized, integration-mad Blacks) to forsake the hundreds of 1,000s of years of Afrikans striving to create the profound theosophical, philosophical, or religious concepts which all Caucasians claim today." The answer is European (and European-American) cultural imperialism; it is a refined tool of oppression! White cultural domination over Blacks continues on its lethal way by falsely insisting that the fictitious Moses is the originator of monotheism. It is clear that Moses is make-believe since he was copied, by Jewish (Hebrew) authors of the Old Testament no earlier than 700 b.c.e., after an Egyptian Christ --Horus--who existed in Egyptian theology more than 1,500 years before Moses (b. 1320 b.c.e.) supposedly lived.

> Middle Kingdom [Dynasties 11-14, ca 2100-1675 b.c.e.] scribes provided a
> Paradise [Heaven] and several Hells. During the [Egyptian] Middle Kingdom the Underworld [Hell, etc.] became a much more frightening place than had been imagined by the authors of the Pyramid Texts [of Dynasty 6]. It was divided into sections, each of which was guarded by fearful monsters. The earliest of the special works which deal with these horrors must date from before the Twelfth Dynasty. One of them, the socalled Book of the Two Ways, is a guide through the subterranean [Underworld] paths.... The second is Spell 336 of the Coffin Texts [of Dynasty 7], which divides up the Underworld journey into a series of obstacles or gates which must be passed through by means of magical formulae. In these early Underworld texts the journey is made by the soul, but in the developed works which appear on the tombs of the New Kingdom [Dynasties 18-23], the theme is the night journey of the sun. As the latter goes through the subterranean ways, it lights up the denizens [inhabitants] of the dark. When the sun passes along it illumines all the forms which must be in the Underworld and belong to the past or future. The temptation to people the darkness with the unredeemed [unreformed, unsaved] dead has appealed to nearly every culture--witness the Underworlds of Homer and Virgil [an ancient Roman author].[21]

> [The first representation, in the history of religion, of hell and heaven] is in the tomb of the father [Pharaoh Seti I, b. 1318 b.c.e.] of Rameses II. It is on this bridge [in the pictorial representation of Seti I's tomb] that the dead person must walk, on this moving bridge, to arrive at paradise [Heaven]. The bridge is actually a serpent, a monster. That dead person is only sustained on the bridge by the quality of his life. After he is judged [by God Osiris in the Underworld], he presents himself before this monster and tries to cross. If he did in life more good than he did harm, he will cross with no problem and is taken in by the gate keepers. So the notion of the immortality of the Soul, was invented by Egypt from the old dynasty [Dynasties 1-10, ca 3200-2150 b.c.e.]. All of these ideas are typically African. It's only in the 2nd century [200 b.c.e.] before [Jesus] Christ that the Old Testament of Judaism adopted definitely the idea of hell and beyond; this was almost 3,000 years after Egypt.[22]

The profound concepts--transmigration, immortality of the soul salvation, monotheism, Heaven, and Hell (the Underworld)--had been created and written (codified) by the ancient Egyptians before Dynasty 7, ca 2270 b.c.e. It is known also that the religious texts of Judaism, Christianity and Islam were not written until 700 b.c.e., 50 c.e., and 670 c.e. respectively (see also Y.A.A. ben-Jochannan, A Chronology of the Bible, pp. 4-5); nevertheless, Western religious teachers (rabbis, ministers, and imams, etc.) have stolen and claimed proudly the Afrikan philosophical and theological principles developed 1,000s of years before those Western (White) religions themselves. Though Western religions did not invent the theological and metaphysical principles they use, Jews, Europeans and Arabs claim evermore proudly Judaism, Christianity, and Islam as their respective cultural (ethnic) concoctions. The Black reader must understand that each ethnic or racial groups builds its esteem by taking pride in its own cultural and religious creations and institutions. Knowing that, I must ask a question: If Negroes in American must worship a god, why would they not select an Afrikan God of the world's first religious system--the ancient Egyptian/Nile Valley Mysteries--from which all other religions sprang (see also Diop, The African Origin of Civilization, p. 287)?

Many Afrikans around the world have been physically oppressed (dominated) and stripped of their cultural and religious institutions by the Slave Trade and European colonialism, neo-colonialism, imperialism and neo-imperialism; presently, Caucasians continue to maintain global supremacy by impressing their cultural and economic system upon the world. As a result, Blacks in the U.S. have no memory of their great Afrikan, historic cultural and religious institutions.

Negroes who insist on worshipping White (Western) religions in spite of the knowledge of Afrikan religions can be described as possessing an oppressed mentality; this mentality is identified typically among a group or class of people that is dominated either numerically, culturally, or economically by another group. Similarly, an analysis by Malcolm X might help the Black reader to understand how Negroes could be content to practice Caucasian religions: Negroes in America are satisfied with the economic (and cultural, religious, etc.) crumbs from the White man's table. Perversely, history-less Negroes in the U.S. attempt to improve their self-image by worshipping White-created gods (e.g., Yahweh; Jesus Christ, etc.) in order to participate in European cultural narcissism (self-adoration); the White psychiatrist Sigmund Freud (in The Future of an Illusion, pp. 12-14) explains that cultural narcissism is the manner by which an elite, upper class in societies has been able to control the suppressed masses.

Before answering a question I posed earlier, I will take this opportunity to clarify what I mean by the terms Black or Blackness. Paraphrasing the mental-giant Haki Madhubuti, Blackness means to possess three characteristics: skin color; the knowledge of one's Afrikan culture and historical consciousness or awareness. Finally, there is a simple reason why religious Negroes in America do not worship an ages-old, Afrikan God (e.g., Amon): Negroes do not consider themselves Afrikan!

> According to archaic [ancient] beliefs, the rain
> was water impregnating the Earth (Mother-

Goddess) sent down by the sky (Father-God, a celestial God who became atmospheric with the discovery of agriculture, according to M. Eliade). The vegetation that grew out of this union was a divine product; whence the idea of a Cosmic Trinity, which, through a series of successive incarnations, would evolve into the Christian Trinity of the Father, Son, and Virgin Mary (later replaced by the Holy Spirit), by way of the Triad Osiris-Isis-Horus.[23] The chthonian-agrarian triad [trio], sky-earthvegetation, in certain countries, such as [ancient] Egypt, eventually became identified as a triad of demi-gods: Osiris-Isis-Horus.[24] Under the names of Osiris, Tammuz, Adonis, and Attis, peoples of Egypt and Western Asia represented yearly decay of the revival of life, especially of vegetable life, which they personified as a god who annually dies and rose again from the dead.[25]

In the developed [Egyptian] theology it was Osiris' soul that was set free.... This god was more than his myth, he was the spirit of life itself, manifest in the sprouting of vegetation and in the seed of animals and men. But the greatest religious achievement of the Egyptians was to take this general fertility god and make him into the saviors of the dead; or, more exactly, the saviour from death. ... [The Pyramid Text of Wenis hymn] may well be the earliest hymn from the Osirian rituals to have survived. This [Dynasty 6, 2420 b.c.e.] text is singularly enlightening as to the fate of Osiris.

'Osiris! you went away but you have returned, you fell asleep, but you have awakened, you died, but you live again.'[26]

... [A] Denderah [A town about 40 miles north of the city Thebes in Upper Egypt] document, however, is amply compensated [accompanied] by a remarkable series of bas-reliefs [sculptures].... These [bas-reliefs] exhibit in a series the dead god Osiris lying swathed as a mummy on his bier [coffinstand], then gradually raising himself up higher and higher, until at last he has entirely quitted the bier and is seen erect between the guardian wings of the faithful Isis, who stand behind him, while a male figure holds up before Osiris' eyes the 'crux ansate,' the Egyptian symbol of [eternal] life. The resurrection of this god could hardly be portrayed more graphically.

In the resurrection of Osiris the Egyptians saw the pledge of a life everlasting for themselves beyond the grave. Egyptians believed that every man would live eternal in the other world [Heaven] if only his surviving friends did for his body what the gods [Isis, etc.] had done for the body of Osiris. Hence the ceremonies observed by the Egyptians over the human dead were an exact copy of those which Anubis, Horus, and the rest [i.e., so-called demi-gods saints, etc.] had performed over the dead god Osiris.

> 'At every burial there was enacted a representation of the divine mystery which had been performed of old over Osiris, when his son [Horus], his sisters [Isis and Nephthys], his friends were gathered round his mangled remains and succeeded by their spells and manipulations in converting his broken body into the first mummy,.... The mummy of an Egyptian deceased was Osiris; the professional female mourners were his two sisters Isis and Nephthys; Anubis, Horus, all the gods of the Osirian legend gathered about the Egyptian corpse.'

Thus every dead Egyptian was identified with Osiris and bore his name.

Thousands of inscribed and pictured tombs that have been opened [sacrilegiously] in the valley of the Nile prove that the mystery of resurrection was performed for the benefit of every dead Egyptian. In an Egyptian text it is said of the departed that 'as surely as Osiris lives, so shall he live also; as surely as Osiris did not die, so shall he not die...'[27]

Concerning the religion of Isis and Osiris; 'No religion had yet brought to men so formal a promise of immortality: this above all gave to the Alexandrian [Egyptian] Mysteries (of Isis) their power of attraction.' These foreign religions which made no distinctions among individuals allowed the disinherited of the plebs [the lower, White classes] to worship. The love of one's neighbor was a moral commonplace in the southern [Afrikan] world: this notion could represent an advance in the morals only in the individualistic northern Mediterranean [i.e., ancient Greece and Rome, etc.]. One cannot too strongly emphasize all that primitive Christianity borrowed from the cult of isis in Rome, even in the structure of its processions. 'Egypt is the country from which contemplative devotion penetrated into Europe.'[28] Worship of the first Virgin Mother (Isis) was common among the ancient Greeks and Romans in Greece and Rome for hundreds [100s] of years before, and up to, the ... Roman Emperor Constantine 'the great' in ca 312 c.e. upon his rise to the throne.

'It has been stated that the religious [i.e., Christianity] of Western Europe as well as Hinduism and Islam of Asia have their foundations in the Egyptian Mystery (Mysteries) System,.... Of course within the 'Black Theology' at the Grand Lodge of Luxor [in ancient Egypt] and this subordinate Lodges was always the teachings about the 'Immaculate Conception] and 'Virgin Birth'.... Jesus, who latter became 'the Anointed/ the Christ,' was definitely only an interpretation [fabrication] from the original story about Isis and Horus.[29] Methodology speaking, Osiris was indeed born the night of December 25th as was Jesus Christ who can be compared to Osiris [who is interchangeable with his son Horus] in this case and in many others.[30]

Horus had two [2] mothers: Isis, the Virgin, who conceived him, and Nephthys, who nursed him. He was brought forth singly and as one of five [5] brothers.

Jesus had two [2] mothers: Mary the Virgin, who conceived him, and Mary, the wife of Cleophas, who brought him forth as one of her children. He was brought forth singly and as one of five [5] brethren.

Horus was the son of Geb, his father on earth.

Jesus was the son of Joseph, the father on earth.

Horus was with his mother, the Virgin, until twelve [12] years old, when he was transformed into the beloved son of God, as the only begotten of the Father in heaven.

Jesus remained with his mother, the Virgin, up to the age of twelve [12] years, when he left her 'to be about his Father's business.

From 12 to 30 years of age there is no record in the life of Horus.

From 12 to 30 years of age there is no record in the life of Jesus.

Horus at 30 years of age became adult in his baptism by Anup.

> Jesus at 30 years of age was made a man of in his baptism by John the Baptist.
>
> Horus, in his baptism, made his transformation into the beloved son and only begotten of the Father--the holy spirit, represented by a bird.
>
> Jesus, in his baptism, is hailed from heaven as the beloved son and only begotten of the Father, God--the holy spirit that is represented by a dove.[31]

The preceding references to Osiris, Isis, and Horus should indicate clearly, to even a most unconscious Negro, the fictitious nature of the Virgin Mary and Jesus. Osiris, Isis, Horus and the doctrines of the Immaculate Conception (Virgin Birth) and resurrected Saviors (Christ) had existed (pre 2420 b.c.e, Dynasty 6) in the Osirian drama of ancient Egyptian theology more than 2,000 years before they were copied or stolen by Christian writers from 50 c.e. onward. I would advise the reader to consult various sources and encyclopedias to research the Nicence Council of Bishops convened by Roman Emperor Constantine in 322 c.e. It was this Nicence Council that adopted finally the doctrine of the Virgin Birth and the divinity of Jesus Christ; additionally, this Council discarded many supposedly unfit books (the Apocrypha or "lost" books) from the Bible (see Y. benJochannan), <u>A Chronology of the Bible</u>, p. 5).

 Surely at some point, the Black reader will wonder about the role of Negro ministers who indoctrinate or brainwash their race with White religion. In spite of the stolen, Egyptian-doctrines of the immaculately born and resurrected Christ, the main participants of the New Testament are in no way Black; I say that knowing that some Black theologians (religious scholars) question the White identity assigned to Jesus Christ. In fact, the pictures of Jesus which Christians worship today are replicas (copies) of the Italian Michaelangelo's cousin. That is, current-day Christians are worshipping reproductions of the individual Michaelangelo was commissioned by Pope Julius 2nd to paint on the ceiling of the Cistene Chapel of St. Peter's Basilica in Rome, Italy in 1509 c.e. Nevertheless, would a mythical, racially-different Jesus alter the

Caucasian cast of characters and orientation of the new Testament? The Black reader <u>must</u> understand that each racial group builds its self-pride by creating and worshipping heroes and religious figures, etc. in its own image!

It is my observation that Negro clergy (ministers) do not consider themselves Afrikans and, therefore, are not interested in worshipping a Black-created God such as Amon of ancient Egypt and present-day West Afrika. Dr. Y.A.A. ben-Jochannan states that Negro ministers and theologians teach the myth of the divinely-inspired Holy Bible in order to control the minds of their congregations and whomever else. However, as the Black reader has seen, the supernatural doctrines of the Bible are not original; and, since the writings of the Old and New Testament scribes are not even original, how can those writings be God-inspired?

> Among the Bedouins [Semites of the Middle East or W. Asia: Jews or Arabs], Mt. Sinai was sacred to the mood god, Sin, from whom it derived its name. Sin, by nature of his nocturnal light, was the favored god of nomadic peoples, their guide and protector at night when they must do most of their wandering in a hot country. Sin was worshipped at Mt. Sinai well into the Christian Era [c.e.]. His symbol was a conical stone surmounted by a gilded crescent.

> When the Israelites [Jews, Hebrews] left their 'Mtn. of the
> Law' [supposedly, after Hebrews left Egypt] they carried with them Sin's commandments to make an altar to burn incense upon, this altar to have 'horns' for a ceremonial blood offering, lavers [large basins for religious washing] for the hands and feet, a tabernacle in which to worship the god and the ritual of burnt offerings. Every seventh ['/th] day, the unlucky day of the mood god [Sin] throughout the East, had become a sabbath or sacred day. The point is that in their [Jewish] own tradition Sinai was the place upon which Yahweh descended with ... all the sacred Law that was the

foundation of Israel, and much of this 'law' was pre-existent in the moon god's cult. Yahweh [Jehovah], slowly taking shape in a welter [mass, turmoil] of polytheism [many gods], took one or another attribute from various of Israel's early gods.

The Pentateuch [the first five books of the Old Testament] is now recognized to stem from three more or less independent sources, the Yahwistic and Elohist versions which were probably not committed to writing before 750 b.c.[e.], and the Priests' Code which was composed as an amplification of [the book of] Deuteronomy.[32] Jews and Christians have tried to explain away certain contradictory details in the order of [the two (2) accounts of] Creation [i.e., Genesis I. 1-II.3 vs. II. 4-22, respectively].... The second Creation account [Genesis II.4-22] implies that the work of Creation occupied a single [1] day. The opening statement [Genesis II.5] recalls several Near eastern cosmogonies [theories of the origin of the universe].

In Genesis II, the name 'Elohim' is combined with a second divine name pronounced Yahweh (usually transcribed as Jehovah, and translated as 'Lord'). The priestly editor [of the 2nd account of Creation: Genesis II.4-22] changed 'Yahweh' to 'Yahweh Elohim' (usually translated as 'the Lord God'). 'Elohim' is the Hebrew variant of the ancient Semitic name for one god of many--Ilu among the Assyrians; Il, or Ilum, among South Arabians; and El among the Hittites.

Many acts attributed in Ugaritic mythology to the bloodthirsty Goddess Anath are attributed in the Bible to Yahweh Elohim. Zachariah (IV.10), and Josephus (Wars V.5.5.) identify the seven branches of the Menorah [a seven-branched candlestick used in Jewish worship] with the seven [7] planetary gods in the Babylonian week to which the order of [the "first"] creation [Genesis I.1-II.3] was tied. Priests were careless about the adaptation of heathen [pagan] sacrificial rites to God's service. The crucial question was: in whose honour these rites should now be enacted?[33]

The city [Babylon] to which Nebuchadrezzar carried off the captives [Hebrews] from Jerusalem was one of the wonders of the Orient. This captivity, or Exile, lasted until [ca] 538 b.c., when the Persians [Caucasians] under Cyrus conquered Babylon, at which time many of the captives [Hebrews] returned to Jerusalem as Persian subjects. Nevertheless certain [Babylonian] story [myth] of the Great Flood, as it was related by Uta-Hapishtim to Gilgamesh, they [the Hebrews or Jews] used with changes in the names and localities as the foundation for an epic of their own. On the [Babylonian] legend [myth] of how the great Bel-Marduk had cut Tiamat in half they [the Hebrews] patterned their own story of creation,.... It was difficult for them [Hebrews] to picture Yahweh in the heavens, so they transferred him to Gilgamesh's land of Eden, the most fertile country in the world according to the Babylonians, one great garden of trees and flowers and fruits. Traders from Persia knew of such a marvelously fertile land: it was on a mountain which they called Pairidaeza or Paradise, and it was here that there grew the Tree of Everlasting Life.

It had been in Eden that Engidu had been created out of clay by Aruru, and had lost immortality by reason of the women whom Shamash had sent to seduce him. They [Hebrews] may have confused

Engidu with the first man, Adapa, or Adamu, as the Babylonians sometimes called him. Or they [Hebrews] may have chiefly remembered [the legendary] Gilgamesh himself, who undertook his epic journey to find the [make-believe] Tree of Knowledge, or Tree of Life--for knowledge and wisdom were equivalent to majic, which was the key to eternal life--only to have a serpent steal it away from him.

Not that these [Babylonian] tales were wholly new: some had been old when [the fictional] Abraham abandoned Ur [Chaldea in Mesopotamia] for Haran [in ancient Egypt]..., as is demonstrated by the fact that two of the Tell el-Armana [of Egypt, Dynasty 18, ca 1370 b.c.e.] letters contain them as school exercises. In the retelling, however, these tales acquired new meaning and became adapted to the God [Yahweh] of Israel.[34]

[Old Testament] Myths of Abram, Sarai, and the Pharaoh; Abram, Sarai, and Abimelech; Isaac, Rebekah, and Abimelech; and, Joseph and Potiphar's wife were borrowed from the Egyptian <u>Tale of Two Brothers</u>.

The Canaanite [pagan] feast of unleavened bread was converted into a commemoration of Israel's [supposed] Exodus from Egypt.[35] Another of the basic religious foundations without which there would be no Judaism or Islam is 'circumcision,' a sacred, social and religious rite in each and every indigenous, traditional African society--including the ancient Nile Valley Africans.... It is to be remembered that in the city of Ur, Chaldea [in Mesopotamia], where [make-believe] Abraham was born, people [Blacks] there were already using the methods of both 'circumcision' and 'excision' which they had adopted from the

> Africans of Egypt and Ethiopia;.... Strangely enough even Abraham's (the first Hebrew or Jew) 'circumcision' made his conversion from alleged 'heathenism' or 'paganism' to 'purity' (Hebrewism); 'circumcision' being one of the most basic ceremonies in a man becoming a Hebrew.[36]

Before beginning my narrative on Judaism, I must give thanks to the High Priest of ancient Nile Valley Mysteries Y.A.A. ben-Jochannan for the knowledge, cited previously in this chapter, concerning the Italian Michaelangelo's Christian artwork in St. Peter's Basilica in Rome (in <u>Our ... Black Clergy without a Black Theology</u>, p. xi). If there were such a thing as God, surely it would have manifested itself in the form of great Black historians, such a Y. ben-Jochannan, C.A. Diop, and Chancellor Williams, etc., who have striven their lifetimes to liberate the mind and bodies of their race.

Although it is said Gilgamesh is listed as an authentic king among ancient Sumerian or Mesopotamian inscriptions, as king Osiris is listed among Egyptian records, his exploits were obviously exaggerated. Actually it is not significant whether Gilgamesh lived; it is significant that the Gilgamesh drama, from which the Jews copied their Creation and Flood stories according to the White scholar Homer Smith, is more than 1,000 years older than the Old Testament.[37]

Apparently, the Jewish writers of the second Creation account (<u>Genesis</u> II.4-22) attempted to combine Elohim, god of the second Creation, with Yahweh, god of the first Creation account (<u>Genesis</u> I.1-II.3), in order to create a more complete, all-powerful god-Yahweh Elohim, translated as Lord God. Elohim would have been the god that Jews carried with them when they left "captivity" in Babylon in 538 b.c.e.; on the other hand, Yahweh was a minor god of the so-called Egyptian pantheon stolen by Jewish scribes in their association with Egypt prior to 750 b.c.e. (ben-Jochannan, <u>Black Man of the Nile</u>, p. 344). All that should not surprise the reader; earlier in this chapter, it was shown that the Hebrew (Jewish) writers of the Old Testament copied the details of the life of Egyptian Horus and transferred those details to the make-believe Moses.

It is appropriate to focus upon the origins and peculiarities of Judaism, Christianity and Islam since Negroes are basking presently in the religious (cultural) sunshine of other ethic (racial) groups. It would appear some Blacks in America have jumped from the religious "frying pan" of Christianity into the cultural "fire" of Islam. According to Y. ben-Jochannan, the Koran (the Islamic Bible) adopts the basic teachings of both the Jewish Old Testament and the Christian New Testament with modifications by the Prophet Mohammed, the Arab founder of Islam. That knowledge should interest the Black reader; this chapter has shown that Jewish and Christian writers of the Testaments stole frequently from the metaphysical concepts, doctrines, ideas and details of the ancient Egyptian Mysteries (Educational) System. Can the Black reader appreciate the present, tragic irony of Negroes being converted to the major Caucasian religions of the West and East (e.g., Buddhism, Confucianism, Zoroastrianism, etc.) when these respective religions have copied and used the theological and theosophical principles created by the ancestors of Negroes themselves. What madness or psychological force could encourage Negroes to forsake a Black-created God--Amon--in favor of Caucasiansponsored Gods--Yahweh, Jesus Christ, or Allah? The answer could be Caucasian religious (cultural) imperialism (domination), which has erased the historical memory and knowledge of Blacks. To add insult to Black injury, respective Western (White) religions profess to be the one and only God-inspired religions while sanctimoniously or hypocritically categorizing traditional Afrikan worship and the ancient mother of religions--the Egyptian Mysteries--as pagan, pantheist, animist, etc.

The reader has seen that the spiritual concepts and supernatural doctrines of the socalled pagan Egyptian Mysteries remain the foundation of present-day Judaism, Christianity and Islam. This knowledge can only disgust Blacks since Afrikans were enslaved, by Europeans and Arabs, and their high-cultures (societies) destabilized and destroyed under the guise (lie) of civilizing and "saving" the souls of Afrikans. Having spoken of paganism, I shall look briefly at the origin of Islam.

The religion of the region of the Arabian Peninsula which spawned Islam was called Sabaeanism; it existed more than 1,000 years before the Arab Prophet Mohammed (b. 570 c.e.) and Islam. Several gods (e.g., Il (El), Ishtar, etc.) of the Sabaeans, Babylonians (in Mesopotamia), and Chaldeans were identical; the reader might recall that, according to the ancient Greek Diodorus, the Chaldeans were originally a colony of Egyptian priests resettled along the Euphrates River. According to C.A. Diop, the Sabaean religion included the 30-day fasting period as in Egypt and the beliefs in an afterlife and sacred springs and stones which continue today in Islam. The Sabaeans (Adites) prayed seven times each day to the sun at different phases of its course; these seven prayers at different hours somewhat resemble Muslim prayers which take place during the same solar phases, but which were reduced by Prophet Mohammed to five compulsory prayers (Diop, The African Origin of Civilization, pp. 126-27)--the other two prayers became optional. The Sabaean (Blacks) practiced already the pilgrimage to Mecca which continued under Islam.

> Mohamet [Arab founder of Islam] triumphantly returned to Mecca. 629
> c.e., a.h. [After the Hejira or flight] 7, was the year Mohamet returned to Mecca from Medina, where he was forced [by the Mecca government] to run and hide. He and his faithful followers [e.g., Bilal--the former Afrikan slave and first convert of Mohammed] of Islam (the 'new religion') adopted Mecca as their 'Holy City.' They also adopted El Ka'aba (A black stone's remains from a meteorite that was imported into Arabia by the Africans of Ethiopia (Abyssinians, when they ruled [defensively] Arabia and Persia, and all the way into India--to the Ganges). But they completely rejected paying any further tribute to the goddess Al'lat, who was replaced by the God Al'lah. Note that the name 'Al'lat' was the origin of the later word 'Al'lah' or 'Supreme God.'
>
> Bilal [Islam's very first high-priest and muezzin or caller to prayer of the faithful] ... was

responsible for the creation of much of what the
Moslems [Muslims], past and present, believe
about 'paradise' (Heaven), also of many of their
first original prayers and doctrines. Bilal saw
'carnal love' as the height of gratification on earth
... [and as the] reward in heaven-Paradise--[which]
he assured for the faithful males of Islam, only.
Bilal promised the faithful [males of Islam] 'Hur-
al-Oyum' (Black-eyed daughters of Paradise;
African virgins) [as their reward in Heaven]....[38]

Chapter 5

Major Western Religions and the Destruction of Afrikan Civilizations

(For my mother, Nadine, and sister, Tonia)

> And this world [of pharaohs, priests, scribes and artists of ancient Egypt], in spite of foreign invasions and political domination, by Greeks and then by Romans, remained more or less intact until the third century A.D. It was Christianity that killed it, in all its aspects. The inevitable conclusion is that Egyptian religion [i.e., the Mysteries] was the heart of the civilization. When that lost its nerve or was superseded the rest fell apart.[1]

> The history of the prolonged Roman difficulties with the Blemmyes [Ethiopians] from the middle of the third century until late in the sixth century A.D. demonstrates ... the hazards associated with the [Roman occupation] ... of Egypt's southern boundaries. Diodorus mentioned the [Roman] problems involved in conducting military operations in Ethiopia.
> At any rate, during the three-hundred [300] year period beginning about 250 A.D., the Blemmyes invaded [Roman-occupied] Egypt again and again and, in spite of Roman repulses and victories, were able to return; ...; for a considerable period they occupied Egypt as far north as Ptolemais ...; they attacked Christian communities and were a constant threat to Roman lives; at times they even allied themselves with the Nobades [Ethiopians], although it was the Nobades [also known as the nobatae, Nobadae, or Nubae] who finally dealt the

blow from which the Blemmyes never recovered. Their [Blemmyes] successes led [Roman emperor] Diocletian [284-305 a.d.] to a decision ... to make a settlement in which he ceded Roman [occupied] territory to the Nobades, neighbors of the Blemmyes, and made an annual payment to both peoples....

Christianity was introduced into Axumite Ethiopia [ancient Punt] in the fourth century [c.e.]. In the fourth and fifth centuries A.D. the Blemmyes consolidated their power in Lower Nubia [ancient Ethiopia, modern-day Sudan].... Within the same period the development of Christianity in [Roman-occupied] Egypt and the introduction of Christianity into Axum had an effect upon the Blemmyes, who, it appears, felt isolated and hemmed in by Christianity. <u>They were the champions of dying [so-called] paganism [i.e., the Nile Valley Mysteries</u>. In the reigns of perhaps both Theodosius II and Marcian (450-457 A.D.) the Blemmyes raided Christian communities.... [Christian] Churches built on the island of Philae [the Nile River first cararact, which represented the ancient boundary between Egypt and Ethiopia] near the [native-born Nile Valley] temples involved in [Roman emperor] Diocletian's ... [pacification] project were being threatened. The Blemmyan [Ethiopian] danger was real; the southern enemies of the Romans were not inglorious warriors.[2]

... The Negroes of Nobadae, the Negroes of Nubia, and the ... [fierce] Blemmyes were in complete control of Upper Egypt, and by religious ties and ... racial affinities had close sympathetic links with the masses [Blacks] of Egypt.[3]

In the sixth century A.D., there was an out-burst of [Christian] missionary activity in Nubia

[ancient Ethiopia]. The Negroes of Nobadae [from the W.
Nubian desert area] were converted to Christianity during the reign of
Justinian (a.d. 527-565), the Roman Emperor of the East. When Christianity spread among the Nobades [or Nobadae], about the middle of the sixth century (ca 540 A.D.), as a result of the competing missionary efforts of Justinian and [his wife] Theodora this people inclined more and more to the Romans and began gradually to [serve as a buffer state between the Roman-occupied Egyptian border and territory and the fierce, traditional Blemmyes].... Taking advantage of the conversion of the Nobades, Justinian concerned himself with the lingering [so-called] paganism at Philae. ... [The Ethiopian Blemmyes had had the] practice of making an annual pilgrimage to Philae [in Egypt] to bring a statue of Isis [Egyptian goddess] from the island to their own land, of using it for religious purposes, and of returning it to Philae. He [Justinian] sent Narses, the commander of the Roman troops in southern Egypt, to Philae, where he closed the Isiac [Isis] shrines, imprisoned the [traditional Afrikan] priests, and had the images of the goddess sent to Constantinople [the capitol of the East Roman Empire in W. Asia]. With the exception of minor episodes, there is no record of further serious attacks from the south [by the Blemmyes against the Roman occupiers] in the sixty century and later.[4]

I would remind the reader again that ancient Ethiopia is the current-day Sudan nation; present-day Ethiopia is the ancient Punt or Abyssinia. The example of White people, such as the ancient Romans, utilizing their cultural institutions, in the form of Christianity, to domesticate and conquer the Ethiopian Nobades and Blemmyes demonstrates concretely the destructive impact of White cultural institutions upon Black people. I have moved from describing the intellectual theft of Afrikan concepts and doctrines, by Judaism, Christianity and Islam, in Chapter Four to catastrophic reality in this chapter: Romans used Christianity to suppress and erase the cultural and national will of the Egyptians and Ethiopians. The Black mental-giant Geo. G.M. James told Blacks in 1954 c.e. (<u>Stolen Legacy</u>, pp. 155, 160) that they should <u>never</u> forget that Roman emperors, including Theodosius and Justinian, used Christianity to destroy the ancient Nile Valley educational and religious (Mysteries) system. Since that is so, why do Negro-Americans not possess that knowledge which Dr. James suggested is crucial to their psychological independence and well-being? Obviously, Negroes do not have their own independent educational system; nor do they have the desire to create one.

Despite Negrophobia or the White scholar's North-east Afrika Syndrome, the Black reader has seen the obvious, from additional evidence above, that the ancient Egyptians and Ethiopians belonged to the same race: Ethiopians, such as the Blemmyes, worshipped the primary Egyptian goddess (or saint, etc.) Isis, whose image was painted Black always (Diop, <u>The African Origin of Civilization</u>, pp. 75-6). Interestingly, the circumstances, of current-day Negro-Americans, resemble somewhat those of the ancient Nobades in Ethiopia. The period of intense conflict between the Nobades and Romans lasted at least 300 hundred years, during which the Nobades fought to maintain their cultural independence before succumbing to the physical and religious domination of the Romans by adopting Christianity finally. Likewise, even though Afrikans (Blacks) were enslaved physically in the U.S., for at least 300 years by European-Americans, some Blacks maintained an independent, rebellious mentality as witnessed by the warriors Gabriel Prosser, Nat Turner, Denmark Vasey, and innumerous insurrections; it was finally the White cultural institution of Christianity which helped permanently to Caucasianize and domesticate Negroes, while displacing the memory and knowledge of their original Afrikan culture. The Black master-historians Chancellor Williams and Y. ben-Jochannan suggest that the effect of Christianity upon Afrikans in America is more destructive than that of their physical subjugation and beatings suffered during the Slave Trade!

Christianity reduces Negroes gladly or willingly to a permanent psychological state, where they can be ruled politically and economically by Europeans or EuropeanAmericans.

Praise must be given to the ancient Ethiopians, such as the Blemmyes, Candace Queens, and Sudanese Pharaohs (e.g., Painkhi, Shabaka, Taharqa, etc.), who fought for 100s of years, beginning in the eight century b.c.e. with their military intercession in Black Egypt against the Assyrians, to protect the physical and cultural independence of the Nile Valley. The reader will recall that the Egyptians fought Caucasian barbarians, for over 1,000 years from the middle of the second millennium b.c.e, until they lost completely their national will in the seventh century b.c.e. after being defeated by the White Assyrians. The Black reader must ask himself or herself a question: Did ancient, medieval, and modern Afrikans fight Arab and European invaders, for 1,000s of years, in order to have their descendants around the world adopt, without struggle, the alien religions and cultures of another race?

> Hebrews (Jews) ... aided the Christians and Moslems in the enslavement of African peoples; at least the Hebrews provided many of the writers who morally justified the enslavement of Africans through their warped interpretations [e.g., the Negrophobic Ham myth] of the Hebrew Torah (Christian Old Testament)--as evidenced in the writings of the sixth century c.e. Babylonian [Jews previously captured in Babylon] Talmudic scholars (see quotations in Black Man of the Nile, by Y. ben-Jochannan, pp. 12-3; from R. Pattai and R. Graves' Hebrew Myths [p. 126]).[5] That Negroes are doomed [due to Old Testament Noah's curse upon Canaan and Ham, i.e., Black people] to serve men of lighter colour was a view gratefully borrowed by Christians [Whites] in the Middle Ages. The Ham myth [in Genesis IX.18-27] is told to justify the Hebrew [Jewish] enslavement of the Canaanites [Blacks]. Noah's

curse [upon Black people] gives mythical validity to a historical situation (slavery).

Abram's [i.e., Abraham--the first Biblical Hebrew] mistrust of the Egyptians [Blacks] as fornicators [supposedly those having sex immorally or outside of marriage] is based on the bad reputation of Ham's descendants: for Misraim (Egypt) figures in Genesis X.6 as a son of Ham. Ham is identified, by a play on words, in Psalms CV.23 and CVI.22, with Kemi, 'black,' a name given to [inhabitants of] Egypt.

The Ham myth was once identical with that of the conspiracy against the shameless [Greek] god Cronus by his sons Zeus, Poseidon and Hades. The Ham myth is related to the Greek myth of how five brothers conspired against their father Uranus. Zeus followed in his father Cronus' example [Cronus had castrated and overthrown his own father Uranus]. The youngest son Zeus castrated Cronus. But Ham's (or Canaan's) castration of Noah has been excised from Genesis.[6]

Can the Black reader appreciate the ingratitude of the Hebrew (Jewish) authors of the Old Testament (Torah, Pentateuch), who, after first stealing their god (Yahweh) and other doctrines and details from the Egyptian Mysteries, racistly cast Canaanites (Blacks) as cursed villains, in order to justify the Jewish theft of Canaan (ancient Phoenicia)? The Old Testament curse began, of course, upon Ham (i.e., Kham, Khem, translated as "Black" in ancient Egyptian), the Biblical ancestor of all Afrikan nations (e.g., Canaan; Kush or Ethiopia; and Misraim or Egypt--see Genesis IX.6-20) and Afrikan people, who were mythically cursed and blackened. The reader should refer to Black Man of the Nile and Hebrew Myths to examine a host of outrageous traits, which have continued to this day, which were falsely attributed to Blacks by the lying and avaricious (thievish) Old Testament writers: Were the

Hebrew authors using "reverse" psychology, to project their own disgusting characteristics upon Black people?

These ancient Jewish mis-scholars appear as Caucasian racists, as described by Dr. Frances Welsing (in <u>The Cress Theory of Color Confrontation and Racism</u>, 1970), reacting psychologically to their numbers inferiority and fear of genetic annihilation in relation to Black people.

Since Judaism, Christianity and Islam adhere to the Negrophobic Ham myth, I must ask the Black reader a question: Why would have self-respecting and raciallyproud Black person subscribe to an obviously anti-Black, Western religion? Likewise, would anyone, except Caucasianized, culturally-insane Negroes, subject their children to Negrophobic theologies or philosophies, which would damage permanently their self-image and self-esteem?

> The 13th and 14th Dynasties were apparently contemporaneous, and Egypt appears to have been divided in two, with two independent kings. We are informed by Jewish historian Flavious Josephus (37-95 a.d.) that during the reign of Timaus, Egypt was invaded by men of ignoble birth who came from the eastern parts [i.e. W. Asia]. These invaders, according to Sir E.A.W. Budge, were Aryans and not Arabs. They founded the 15th
> Dynasty, and their first king was Salatis [These Hyksos invaders ruled the Nile R. delta or Lower Egypt]. Ahmes, the third son of Seqenenra 3rd, was finally responsible for the expulsion of Hyksos from Egypt. Ahmes I became the first ruler of the 18th Dynasty. He reigned for about 25 years, and we know that he carried his fight against the Hyksos right into Palestine [Phoenicia].[7]
>
> In [ancient] Syria [the country between Egypt and Mesopotamia] the Bedouins were mostly nomadic

shepherds, perpetually quarreling with each other for the rights to the most fertile wadies and the permanent springs, and Egyptian and Mesopotamian records reveal that they were

given to harassing important trade routes between the Nile and Euphrates. ... A people known to the Sumerians as the Habiru were living in southern Mesopotamia; they were not Sumerians, but Aramaean [Syrian] nomads who came in from the desert to enroll as mercenaries with the Sumerians.[8] [The mythical] Abraham, an Aramaean patriarch, entered Palestine [Canaan] with the Hyksos hordes early in the second millennium b.c. [9] When or why any of [the legendary, first Hebrew] Abraham's descendants entered Egypt is unknown. They may have been among the Semitic mercenaries or servants who accompanied the Hyksos when this hated people first brought ruin upon Egypt. Throughout this period [the rule of the Shepherd Kings in Lower Egypt 1675-1600 b.c.e.] and later, famine, war in Syria and the expansion of Mesopotamian cities all conspired to drive westward not only isolated individuals but whole families and tribes.[10]

The Jewish historian Flavius Josephus states that many Jews left Egypt when the Hyksos were driven out, and he actually refers to the Book of Exodus. Josephus says that Israelites numbered 600,000 men, not counting women and children. There is a great deal of controversy about Josephus' [ca 37-95 c.e.] narrative.[11] Whether any such mass exodus account that there went out of Egypt 'about 600,000 on foot that were men, beside children. and a mixed multitude went up also with them; and flocks, and herds, even very much cattle.' Apart from the 'mixed multitude,' this would mean 1,500,000 men, women and children, and an equal number of cattle and sheep, and any such mass movement would certainly have resounded loudly in Egyptian or Syrian history. it is more likely that the legend of the exodus is a garbled and fanciful account of the flight from Egypt to Palestine [Phoenicia, Canaan] of a relatively few members of the Rachel [Hebrew] tribe under the leadership of a patriarch who fled the country because he had come afoul of the Egyptian law; or perhaps it only reflects the econtinuous infiltration of Hebrews into and out of Egypt over the period between the Hyksos invasion [1675 b.c.e.] ... and the reign of Merneptah [Pharaoh Rameses 2's successor who ruled 1232-1224 b.c.e.], and their gradual rise to power in Palestine. Later, when they were politically established in that country, their Egyptian experiences and the adventures which they had had at one point in their travels were developed into a tale of epic proportions.[12]

Rameses 2 allegedly chased '... Moses from the city of Soccoth to Rameses ...,' etc. All of this was supposed to have taken place around c. 1298-1232 b.c.e., during the 19th dynasty, the period when Rameses reigned over Egypt and other nations in the Nile Valleys. One must remember that there is no other records than the Hebrew or Jewish Holy Torah to justify the existence of the Biblical figure named 'Moses,' and or the stories attributed to him. The sole source of the Exodus (Passover story), in the so-called 'Five Books of Moses' or 'Holy Torah,' by the Hebrews or Jews, is without any corroboration of any of the writers who lived in Egypt and all other nations bordering on Egypt during the period this alleged historical drama took place.

The so-called 'Exodus' drama in the Second Book of Moses (Holy Torah or Old Testament) was

> never mentioned in Ta-Merrian [ancient Egyptian] history by indigenous African scribes of Ta-Merry. The most recent excavations in the area of Ta-Merry, where the monumental drama of the 'Exodus' allegedly took place, have not proven that this major event ever occurred in the manner indicated in the Five Books of Moses at any time in Ta-Merrian history. One should notice that it was contrary to the common practice of the indigenous Africans of the High-Culture of Ta-Merry and other Nile Valley nations not to have recorded as significant an event as the Haribu ('Jews') leaving Ta-Merry ['land of the inundation;' Egypt] in such a mass migration ('Exodus') as depicted in the Second Book of Moses...[13]

Perversely, it is Caucasianized, mis-educated Negro ministers who spearhead the cultural and psychological genocide of Blacks, by contaminating them with the Negrophobic or racist Exodus and Ham myths, respectively. From an unemotional position, the Old Testament, instead of appearing as an original, divinely-inspired, errorless text, can be viewed as the effort of Jewish theologians to construct a cultural (sociohistorical) document and religion worthy of uniting their particular ethnic group. If the Negro clergy were not so intent upon controlling the minds of their congregations with myths and supernatural stories, they could explain that original cultural and religious institutions have been the necessary and normal manifestations of any independent and creative race; consequently, Blacks could exert themselves to rediscover their original Afrikan culture and religion (i.e., the Ta-Merrian Mysteries, which created the first Black Bible--<u>The Book of the Coming Forth by Day and by Night</u>), instead of copying an already forged Western (White) religion.

The respective, Negrophobic Exodus and Ham myths combine to reveal the racist intellect of the Judaistic authors. Obviously, the reader must regard the Five Books of Moses (Moses supposedly lived 1200 b.c.e.) with complete disbelief, given the nonexistence of Biblical texts predating the 8th century b.c.e. In the absence of real documents, common sense and simple arithmetic expose the impossibility of 8th century b.c.e., Hebrew scribes describing supposed events which occurred 500 to 3,000 years earlier, as written in the Old Testament (Torah, Pentateuch, Five Books of Moses, etc.).

I do not think it necessary to comment further upon the Negrophobic, Jewish exodus myth: The Exodus antagonists (villains) are Black Egyptians, while the protagonists (heroes) are semitic (Caucasian) Hebrews. However, I would add some details undergirding my observation that the racist Ham story was copied from an earlier Greek fable. It has been stated previously that the onset of Greek culture can be dated to 15th and 16th century b.c.e. Egyptian seals on documents located in Greece; on the other hand, the name "Israel" appeared for the first time in history on a stela (an inscribed stone slab) constructed during the rule of Pharaoh Merneptah (ca 1232-1224 b.c.e.) to commemorate his defensive was in Palestine, W. Asia (see Y. ben-Jochannan, <u>Black Man of the Nile</u>, p. 236-37; Diop, <u>African Origin of Civilization</u>, p. 213). The Greeks are recognized generally as the first civilized Caucasians and Homer (ca 881 b.c.e.), as the first literate Caucasian. Since ancient Blacks (Egyptians) educated the barbaric Greeks before educating the equally barbaric Hebrews, does it not reason that the Greek myth, of Zeus' betrayal of his father Cronus, fathered the racist Jewish story of Ham's "betrayal" of his father Noah?

> In the latter part of the sixth century [c.e.], shortly after the death of [Roman] Emperor Justinian, the story of the great Arab-Moorish civilization begins with the birth of Mohammed in the year 571. Mohammed brooked no opposition, challenging all dissenters to mortal combat, and saying boldly:
>
>> 'I, the last of the prophets, am sent with the sword. let those who promulgate my faith enter into no argument or discussion but slay all who refuse obedience to the law. Whoever fights for the true faith, whether he fall or conquer, will assuredly receive a glorious reward.'

Islamic conquests, following the death of Mohammed in 632 a.d., were remarkable for their rapidity of accomplishment. The first invasion of Africa occurred in 640 a.d., . . . and by the year 642 Egypt was another province of the expanding Moslem domains. In No. Africa, Islamic armies met stiff opposition, but by 672 a.d. they had overrun Tunisia..[14]

'It is not true to say that they [Islamic Arabs] carried all before them immediately; they met with fierce resistance and were more than once driven back. But history has largely forgotten the details of the struggle; the magnitude of the final success has obliterated the unsuccessful opposition of No. Africa [Blacks] to its new [Arab] rulers.'

In 681 a.d. Oqbar-ben-Nafi continued the conquest still further westward and on to the Atlantic seaboard. The indigenous inhabitants of No. Africa, finding the rapacity and greed of Arabs equal only to those of the Romans, Greeks, and Vandals, decided to rise up against Arab rule. North Africans [Blacks] rallied under the banner of one Kuseila and defeated and killed by fresh Arab forces. Kuseila's position as a leader of African resistance was quickly taken up by a relative--a woman named Dahia-al-Kahina. Under her leadership Africans fought back valiantly and drove the Arab army into Tripolitania.

'Arab general, Hassan-bin-Numan, was successful in capturing Carthage in 698 a.d. But his victory was short-lived, for Kahina, rallying the African forces once more, drove Hassan from the city. The position was becoming desperate, however, and Queen Kahina order a terrible devastation [scorched-earth policy] of fertile districts of Byzacine ... [to] deter Arabs from returning.

> Queen Kahina was finally defeated and slain by Hassan-bin -Numan in 705 a.d.[15]

> After Queen Kahina's death, the Arabs began to change their strategy in advancing their faith and power in Africa; a partnership was established between Africans and Arabs that would last 300 years after Queen Kahina stopped the southward spread of Mohammedanism into the West Sudan.[16]

The warriors Queen Kahina and King Kuseila would spit on modern-day integrationist Negroes; North Afrikan Blacks, who fought for 65 years (640-705 c.e.) against Arab land expansionism in the name of "saving" souls to Islam, would not appreciate the Caucasian religion Islam either. Islamic Arab imperialism, beginning in the 7th century c.e. and continuing in the 11th century, explains the racial composition of current-day No. Afrika (i.e., Egypt, Sudan, Libya, Tunisia, Algeria, Morocco, Mauritania), in the same manner that European-Americans occupy the stolen Indian empire called America.

Additionally, 7th century, Islamic-Arab greed and aggression explains an apparent contradiction in Black behavior that I mentioned in the war chronology, given in the Introduction: Islamized, Afrikan Moors (Blacks) provided the bulk of the military muscle that allowed Arabs to attack and control Spain and Portugal, from the 8th until the 15th century c.e.

A most prominent characteristic of white Arab culture has been military feudalism (Diop, <u>The Cultural Unity of Black Africa</u>, p. 97); is it any wonder that North Afrikans, Islamized by invading, 7th century Arabs, would be infected with a war-like mentality (e.g., General Tarik who conquered Spain in 711 c.e.)? A basic premise of this work, as adopted from C.A. Diop's Two-Cradle Theory, is that Caucasians (including Semitic Arabs) have developed deeply-entrenched patriarchal, xenophobic, and war-like traits, resulting from 1,000s of years of nomadic existence in inclement Europe and Asia. Given that premise and the destructive acts of Caucasians (e.g., the "Asiatics," Hyksos, "BarBar," "Lebou," "Palestious," Achaeans, Assyrians, Persians, Greeks, Romans, etc.) invading Afrika, does it surprise the Black reader that white Arabs, in the name of their cultural institution Islam, displaced, oppressed and killed the original, Black inhabitants of No. Afrika, in the same way that Europeans annihilated and displaced the indigenous inhabitants of North America?

As the reader shall see soon, the No. Afrikan Moors of the "Early Ages" (700-1100 c. e.) would not be the only Black de-cultured or disoriented by the White cultural institution Islam. The great historian J.G. Jackson (<u>An Introduction to African Civilizations</u>, pp. 188-89) maintains that the word "Moor" (i.e., "Maurus," "Mauri," or "mauron") means "Black" literally (see also F.M. Snowden, <u>Blacks in Antiquity</u>, pp. 114). Additionally, the classical scholar F. Snowden says the Mauri (Moors) were described, by Greeks and Romans, as "nigri" (black) and "adjusti" (scorched) and that Greeks interpreted "nigrum" (black) as "mauron" (see <u>Before Color Prejudice</u>, pp. 9, 113). If the Black reader would take a moment to discuss the etymology (origin) of that word. Perhaps European-American sources are confused about the ethnicity (race) of the Moors since the Moors are associated with establishing a flowering civilization of arts and sciences in Spain, which included W. Europe's fist university at Salamanca.[17]

> In 1020 [c.e.] some of the African [Black] tribes around the Senegal River [in W. Afrika], and the areas immediately to the north came together with the sole object of checking the growing power of the Ghana Empire. They appointed as their leader a chief from the Lemtuna tribe whose name was Tarsina. Tarsina embraced the Islamic faith and changed his name of Abdulla Abu Mohammed. In 1020 North African forces with Arab assistance attacked the [Ghana] Empire, but were driven back. Having failed to win large numbers of the inhabitants of the Senegal and the areas bordering on the Sahara desert by preaching, Ibn Yasin [the religious leader chosen by Yahia Ibn Ibrahim, the son-in-law of chief Tarsina, to teach the Koran to his people] resolved to achieve his objective by force.

In 1042, with the zeal of a fierce reformer, he left his monastic retreat [on a small island in the Senegal R.] and led his followers [the Almoravids made attacks on some of the outlying districts. These [Almoravid] monks, the former inhabitants of the monastery, won victory after victory, and soon their army was 30,000 strong.

Bassi [the aged Emperor of Ghana] had always remained on good terms with the Moslems, but had himself refused to give up the ancient worship, a fact which had not pleased the Almoravids, who were out to conquer the world for an austere Islamic faith. In 1076, the blow that destroyed the Ghana Empire fell with shattering force. Almoravide forces under Abu Bekr [the brother of Yahia ibn Ibrahim] captured and sacked the city [the capitol city Koumbi-Koumbi], and this brought about the dismemberment of the Ghana Empire.

The victory [at Koumbi-Koumbi, the capitol of Ghana] of Abu Bekr and his Almoravid forces in 1076 was a high-water mark in West African history. It resulted in the southward march of several tribes, including the Akan group--the Ashantis, Fantis, Akims, Akwapims, Akwamus, and Gyamans. The Akans today live roughly 1,000 miles southwest of their original home. They appear to have begun their long march southward as one political unit, bound together by common ties of language and custom; but by the time they arrived on the borders of the Gold Coast divisions had developed--divisions which have survived to this day. The Akans had been used to savannah lands in their former home, but now they had to live in a forest belt. Formerly they had used the plough for cultivating the land; but ... The plough could no longer be employed. Cattle and horses could not survive there, and even today it is not unusual to find Akans who have never seen a horse or a cow. The effect of the tsetse fly was to make it impossible for the Akans to practice agriculture at the high level to which they had been accustomed in the Ghana Empire.

The Akans left the northern savannah regions of the Ghana Empire in 1076 [c.e.]. There is little doubt that the Akan people migrated from somewhere in the Ghana Empire: the customs and traditions of the people give convincing proof of this. All accounts show that the customs in ["medieval"] Ghana approximate to the Akan customs of today. 'Motherright' [matriarchy] prevailed in the city [Koumbi-Koumbi], and people were succeeded by their sisters' children. There was also the traditional unwillingness to accept Islam, as noticeable among the Akans of today as in Ghana some 900 years ago.[18]

The Islamization of W. Africa began with the Almoravidia movement [consisting primarily of Black Muslims] in the tenth century. It can be emphasized that it introduced a sort of dividing line in the evolution of religious consciousness, first of the princes, and as a result, among the people. The traditional [Afrikan] religion withered away little by little under the influence of Islam, as did the mores and customs.[19] The king [in those places in Black Afrika where the people and king became Islamized] was no longer a preacher; the Halo of Holiness which surrounded him was progressively to fall onto the shoulders of representatives of the foreign religion (a Muslim clergy of lower-class origin). What had created his spiritual force, was the traditional religion; that along with the cosmogony, justified his place in society. When those [the traditional, Afrikan religion and cosmogony] were overcome by the 'foreign' religion, the same fate would befall the institutions [e.g., matriarchy] to which they had given rise.

Bakri [an Arab historian who visited Ghana, W. Afrika] relates that the king's interpreters were often chosen from among the Muslims likewise, the steward of the Treasury and the majority of the viziers [executive officers]. There is then every reason to believe that in 1067 a.d., at a time [Al] Bakri wrote, the Islamization of Ghana, though still only very slight, had already influenced its political customs. The same must also have been true in Mali [a great, medieval W. Afrikan empire], and Ibn Khaldun [an Arab scholar who visited Mali] gives the name of its first Islamized king, Bermendana. The political constitution of Songhai [a great, 16th century empire], as it is revealed through the text of the Tarikh es Sudan, shows an identical situation. Songhai, which belongs to the last phase of Islamization of 16th century Africa, had political customs less imbedded in tradition. They in every way resemble those which applied in the Caliphates of Baghdad [Iraq] and courts of the Arab Orient. the same endless intrigues took place around the throne. The provincial governors were mere civil servants, dismissable at any moment, in Songhai.

The second period of Islamization was marked by the conversion of people whether through the automatic imitation of their chiefs, or through some violent action of these chiefs, sometimes going beyond their borders and becoming veritable Holy Wars: all such Holy Wars were conducted by Black chiefs.

The Askia Mohammed on his return [from the holy land Mecca] undertook the first important

Holy War waged by a Black sovereign. The enemy was the [traditionalist] Mossi emperor Nasere (August 1497-August 1498). The <u>Tarikh-es-Sudan</u> relates that Askia Mohammed subdued all peoples 'as far as Teghezza, by fire and sword.' Askia Mohammed was the monarch whose attitude coincided with the completion of the Islamization of the Songhai monarchy.

'it is notable that, in Mossi country where the African tradition remained in effect, only one case of political conflict around the succession to the throne is cited, in the whole history of Mossi [W. Afrika], although it is longer than that of Songhai.

One might term as 'Sherifism' the irresistible impulse on the part of most Muslim chiefs of Black Africa to link themselves to the family tree of Mahomet. Such legends have proliferated in Black Africa since Islam came in and have contributed to altering the authentic history of the continent.

'Consciousness of the continuity of the [Afrikan] people's historical past has been progressively weakened by [foreign] religious influences. Beginning with the 7th century, the history of that region [i.e., the Nile Basin] appeared as if polluted by the image of the Pharaoh, the Biblical curse on whom is perpetuated in Islam. Islam, ..., takes no account of the traditional past. The [Islamic] equivalent of the Western pagan past must be hushed up, renounced, permanently forgotten. Reasons such as these explain why today the Blacks of Khartoum [in present-day Sudan] have a sense of shame at acknowledging their relationship to the ancient past of Meore [a city of ancient Ethiopia]. The ruins from that period, the temples of Semna, Meroitic writing, all of this is of no interest because it is tainted with a pagan tradition that no good Muslim would think of recalling.[20]

Earlier I have documented the Roman use of Christianity to domesticate and divide and conquer the Nobade and Blemmye Ethiopians; would the Black reader agree that we have just seen other prime examples of the disastrous effect of a Caucasian cultural institution, in the form of Islam, upon Afrikan civilizations? At this moment, in the examination upon Afrikan people, surely only a "blind," Black Muslim could fail to see the disorienting and destabilizing influence of Islam upon Black civilizations of the Early and Middle Ages (ca 700-1500 c.e.). Consider the following:

1. Fanatical, Caucasianized Almoravides waged "holy" wars to conquer "pagan"
Ghana, W. Afrika. Islam was the incentive for Almoravid Blacks to attack and destabilize their own race and high-cultures. Historian J.C. de-Graft Johnson's description of the permanent dismemberment of the W. Afrikan Akan group is not a myth or an isolated event; Islam and the Arabs and, later, Christianity and the Europeans would totally dispute the material and socio-political life of Blacks and, thereby, prevent the formation of continent-wide, multinational territories in modern Afrika.

2. Islamized Afrikan chiefs killed traditionally religious (pagan) members of their own race in an effort to convert them and "save" their souls. Of course, the Islamization of W. Afrika ensured the economic welfare of Arabs; e.g., the 14th century Mali ruler Musa, during his pilgrimage to the Islamic holy-land Mecca, bestowed so much gold (300 lbs.) upon Arab merchants that it took the Middle East market 12 years to re-stabilize. A discussion of Islamized, Black rulers converting the Afrikan population violently and modern-day calendars, distributed by various European-American beer companies, depicting famous Afrikan "heroes," raise the questions of how and which ancestors should be chosen by Blacks as heroes. For example, who should be glorified by Afrikans (Blacks) as a hero--the well-renown, Islamized Songhai ruler Mohammed Ture, who proselytized (converted) his 16th century brothers at sword-point, or the great Mossi king Nassere, who fought Mohammed Ture to a standstill

to maintain the cultural integrity of his people, and the most powerful, 15th century c.e. chief Sonni Ali who despised Islam and resisted the Islamization of his Songhai empire?

3. The disorienting psychological influence of Islam upon Blacks encourages Afrikan chiefs to claim racial descent from the family of the Arab Mahomet. As a perpetuator of the Negrophobic, Old Testament curse upon Egyptians, Islam brainwashes Black Muslims to reject their great, traditional (so-called pagan) past, which predates Islam by 1,000s of years.

Does it sicken the Black reader to consider the disastrous effect of the Arab religion Islam upon Afrikans? Even given the loss of the more theoretical mathematics and sciences and writing, which were created in ancient Egypt, it should pain the Black reader to imagine how socially, politically, and materially advanced Africa would be if unimpeded by foreign cultural institutions and unending Caucasian invasions, which began in ca 2250 b.c.e. according to Egyptian texts (Diop, African Origin of Civilization, p. 205).

While original hieroglyphics and cursive have been documented among the W. Afrikan Blacks of Sierre Leone and the Cameroon (Diop, Precolonial Black Afrika, p. 185, 188-89), medieval Afrikans lost the need for extensive written communication, once ancient Egypt was destroyed, and resorted to developing their socio-political structures, instead of building immense material structures like those in Egypt (African Origin of Civilization, pp. 159-60).

Given the destruction of African culture by Islam and the Arabs from 640 c.e. to the present, it is completely astounding that Afrikan-Americans would adopt the Caucasian, cultural institution Islam. Historian Y. ben-Jochannan says Blacks have rushed to claim Islam and Arabic heritage in their struggle to rid themselves of Judeo-Christian, religious enslavement in America.

> With the coming of Islam [in Afrika], that is to say, under the influence of an exterior factor, and not by an internal evolution, most of the people who in the Middle Ages were matrilineal became patrilineal, at least in appearance. This is how the patrilineal regime, gradually and progressively

became substituted for the matrilineal regime, from the tenth century onwards. In West Africa, the adoption of the father's name for the children seems to stem from this same Arabic influence; as a matter of fact, we have just learnt from [13th century Black Muslim scholar] Ibn Batouta that in 1253, children took than name of their maternal uncle, ..., but the regime was purely matrilineal; it only ceased to be so from the time when, according to Islamic custom, the name of the father was substituted for that of the uncle. 'According to native traditions it was the Bambara who first, in the Sudan, broke with this [matrilineal] practice and it is from this that they derive their name--Ban-ba-ra or Ban-ma-na meaning separation from the mother--... In our times male kinship or consanguinity persists among the Bambara and has gained the upper hand among the Sarakolle and among part of the Mandingos or Malinke; ....

It is found that the present tendency, of the internal evolution of the African family, is towards a patriarchy, more or less, attenuated by the matriarchal origins of the society. We cannot emphasize too much the role played in this transformation by outside factors, such as the religions of Islam and Christianity and the secular presence of Europe in Africa.

The African who has been converted to Islam is automatically ruled, at least as far as his inheritance is concerned, by the patriarchal regime. It is the same with the Christian, whether Protestant or Catholic. But in addition, [European] colonial legislation tends everywhere [in 1959 c.e.] to give official status to these private choices...[21]

Is the Black reader sickened sufficiently by the disastrous influence of Islam and foreign cultural institutions upon Afrikan culture yet? Certainly, the Black female reader will be sickened to consider that women, prior to 1880 c.e. in polygamous, Islamized Afrika, were sometimes treated as beasts of burden and exploited economically, according to the great Black historian Walter Rodney (How Europe Underdeveloped Africa, p. 226). This chapter aimed to examine the destructive effect of Caucasian, cultural institutions upon Black (Afrikan) societies. Does it affect the thinking, of the Black, to know that Islam initiated jihads (holy wars) in 12th century East Afrika and that the greedy Arabs invaded North Afrika, for the second time, in the 11th century; enslaved millions of 14th and 15th century, Central and Southeast Afrikans; and wreaked havoc in 18th and 19th century, West and Central Afrika?

The reader has seen that it was in the traditional, medieval state Mossi that matriarchy (uterine or matrilineal succession) ensured the stable and legitimate transmission of social and political rights among Afrikans, as opposed to the turbulent, patrilineal-controlled, Islamized W. Afrikan empires. Matriarchy did not interfere with the development of a modern economy in early and medieval Afrika: There was a modern form of commercial activity covering all Black kingdoms; there were entire merchant classes in the empires of Ghana, Mali, Songhai, and Monomotapa (Diop, Precolonial Black Afrika, pp. 131-32). Pagan Ghana, W. Afrika and Monomotapa, E. Afrika were modern-like, international trading powers and the process of "detribalization" was complete prior to the Islamization of 11th century Ghana (Diop, Cultural Unity of Black Africa, pp. 69-70).

Any theory aside, matriarchal, Afrikan societies insure that there are no orphans or impoverished widows and women since the social responsibility and rights of particular matriarchal family or clan rest with the maternal uncles. Does part of the future salvation of modern Afrikan civilization rest with an updating, of the matriarchal principle, of traditional Black societies, such as the Ashantis, Yorubas, Peuls, and serers of W. Afrika; the Bantu of Central Afrika; and the "Swazi" and "Twsana" of So. Afrika, etc.?

The impact of matriarchy and "detribalization" upon indigenous Afrikan economic production is surely an area of Black studies worthy of the attention Afrikan females!

> Proselytizing through military force (armed violence), as employed European colonialists--the so-called Christian missionaries included-during their six [6] 'Crusades' in Africa and Asia, has never been done by any [traditional] African religious group under the pretense of following their 'scriptures.' For example: As powerful as the Empire of Ethiopia once was, even to the point of expanding [defensively] her ... empire to the Ganges R. in India, Asia she did not force her religion upon the Indian people she conquered.[22]
>
> Christianity suppressed slavery, but the Christians of the 16th century reestablished it, as an exception, indeed to their social system, and restricted to one of the races [i.e., Blacks] of mankind.[23] The records show that Henry's [i.e., Portugese Prince Henry the Navigator] captains, ..., called at Rio d'Ouro [W. Afrika] in 1441 and brought back with them to Portugal some gold dust and ten Africans whom Prince Henry handed over as slave gifts to the Pope, who there and then conferred to Portugal the right of possession and sovereignty over all lands to be discovered to the East of Cape Blanco. When Pope Martin 5th received the first slave gifts brought from Africa by Henry's captains, henry was assured of Papal support for the slave trade. Great was the rejoicing in Lisbon [Portugal] as each succeeding batch of African slaves arrived. Holy men of the day professed to see in the slaves men and women in the highest sense free, since, one fettered in [so-called] heathenism, they now enjoyed the liberty of Christianity.[24] [Likewise,] The planter [i.e., 17th-19th century c.e. Europeans, in the W. Indies and the U.S.] looked upon slavery as eternal,

ordained by God, and went to great lengths to justify it by scriptural [Biblical] quotations.[25]

Religious history tends to have a political bias in the long run. We find modern Negrophobes like Dr. Stoddard urging Christianity upon Africans. Dr. Stoddard continues significantly [he was writing in 1920]: 'Certainly, all white men, whether professing Christians or not, should welcome the success of missionary efforts in Africa. In so far as he is Christianized, the Negro's savage instincts will be restrained and he will be disposed to acquiesce in white tutelage (Lothrop Stoddard, The Rising Tide of Colour, pp. 96-7).' Henri Junod (a Protestant missionary) has the reputation of being an objective ethnographer, and this is what he writes: 'Christianity alone will make out of the Black a servant satisfied with his lot, for it alone can bring him to a free and voluntary submission to the plans of Divine Providence.... (H. Junod, Ba Ranga, p. 482)'[26]

If there is anything more astounding than Afrikan-Americans adopting the Arabic religion Islam, it is Negroes clinging to the European cultural institution Christianity. Christianity forms a major component of the cultural armament of Europeans and European-Americans, whose domination and enslavement of Blacks in Africa exceeded even that of the greedy Arabs. Even though Dr. Y. ben-Jochannan says Afrikan-American Muslims do not recall the destructive history of Islam and the Arabs in Afrika, it is obvious that Muslim Afrikan-Americans have not lost all their common sense and intelligence: For example, Brother Silis Mohammed (in The Wake of the Nation of Islam, p. 186) says that "... a mystery god or a mystery Allah will not protect you against thieves, wrongdoers or the wicked. Nor will a mystery god, Allah, defend you when you are under attack or abuse." Similarly, psychologist Sterling Plumpp warns Negro Christians and Afrikan traditional religionists: "The [helpless, fearful] attitude we develop about God is the same attitude we adopt concerning our [socio-political] environment. The gods didn't stop the white boy and gun powder when they brought our forefathers over here [America],.... I say it makes no different what God you call upon if you are a slave, because if you don't free yourself, you don't get freed (Black Rituals, pp. 52, 63, 71)."

My sole intent in this text has not been to ride upon a high academic "horse." With the continued hope of making myself clear about the catastrophic relationship between Western, narcotizing (i.e., religious) institutions and Black people, I would like to quote briefly the intense Brother S. Plumpp:

> 'At the base of all religion in the West is a class of priests, shamans, emans, etc., ... who decipher for the masses what reality is and ought to be. The problem of Black people all over the world is that their intellectuals [i.e., independent, Afrikan-centric thinkers] have never had real power within their own Black communities because they have been a threat to the preacher elite who knows what the Truth is. It seems that the diverse and uncooperative nature of the [Christian] churches makes them more of a tribal problem for Black Africans in America than there are for the different tribes in the Motherland. If Black churches are unable to establish alternative [Afrikan-centric] educational systems and to be a leadership force independent of the [White] mainstream, then the Black church no longer has a function in Black life (Black Rituals, pp. 40-45, 63, 74).'

The Black reader might suppose that many Negroes have not been exposed to the information contained in this text; however that may be, European, cultural (i.e., political, educational, philosophical, religious, etc.) domination of Blacks ensures that the European psychiatrist Sigmund Freud's analysis of oppressed mentalities is accurate.

> 'In spite of their [the underprivileged, suppressed classes] hostility to them [the favored, ruling, White classes], they may see them in their

> ideals;.... On the strength of ... differences every culture claims the right to look down on the rest [i.e., foreign cultures]. ... The [narcissistic] right to despise the people outside it [a particular cultural unit or society] compensates the [the suppressed classes] for the wrongs they suffer within their own unit (S. Freud, <u>The Future of an Illusion</u>, p. 13).'

 First, as a result of military and economic domination, and, now cultural domination (imperialism), Afrikan-Americans have internalized the ideals, values, and beliefs of European-Americans and consider their oppressed status in America more desirable than the condition of all other Blacks on this planet!

> "Here we are at the very heart of the 'race problem'--this self-abnegation, self-effacement, the loss of self-identity by cutting their roots with the [Afrikan] past and thereby losing the very links with their history from which a people draws strength, inspiration to move forward to even higher ground and, in fact, the reason for being. In short, in the incongruous attempts to replace his own values with those of the white man, the black man lost his own [Afrikan] personality and therefore, his manhood--almost absolutely (C. Williams, <u>The Destruction of Black Civilization</u>, p. 266)."

Chapter 6

The Glory of Medieval or Precolonial (Pre-European), Black Afrikan Nation-States and their Destruction by Arabs and
Europeans (and European-Americans.)
(To the memory of Chancellor Williams)

> Africa, in the eyes of [European-centric] specialists, is depicted as a land which prior to colonization was only at the level of a subsistence economy: the individual, virtually crushed by the forces of nature. No creation, no activity reflecting a society freed from material constraints might be found there. Exchange relationships, were governed by barter. Notions of money, credit, stock market, thrift, or the accumulation of wealth by individuals belong to a type of commerce connected with a higher economic organization: they could not have been found at the alleged level of African economy. This opinion arose from a preconceived idea of African societies: they had to be specifically primitive, therefore endowed in every respect with the systems characteristic of such a condition.[1]

One way of judging the level of economic development in Africa five centuries [500 yrs.] ago is through the quality of products. Africa had elements of the guild system The guild marked an intermediate stage between domestic production and the factory system. In a few places in Africa, the economy was far removed from simple barter and subsistence. As a part of the extension of trade in every part of the African continent between the 10th and 15th centuries, it was noticeable that barter was giving way to some forms of money exchange.[2]

It was therefore, not a matter of backward peoples unable to conceive and produce coins of gold or other metals, for, ..., such coinage was very widespread in [medieval] Black Africa at the time. As for gold dust, a conventional quantity of approximately 4.6 grams (probably more often measured than weighed) constituted what was called the 'mitkal' of gold dust; this was the gold standard, in the strictest modern sense of the term, on the basis of which minted coins (whose composition might be adulterated with non-precious metals), as well as cowries, was worth anywhere from 500 to 3,000 cowries [shells], available [Arabic] documents inform us. Thus these (Arabic) documents allow us to be sure of the use in Arab Africa of the imprinted gold coins. So there existed in W. Africa a whole gamut of currencies usable according to the value of the goods purchased. A remark by Ibn Haukal attests to the use of the acknowledgment of debts in writing: he saw a text in which an inhabitant of Sijilmasa [a city in Arab-occupied No. Afrika] acknowledged his indebtedness to a citizen of Aoudaghast [pre-Islamized Ghana, W. Afrika] in the sum of 40,000 dinars. To the author of The Book of Roads and Kingdoms, such an occurrence was unique in the trading world of the tenth century. Even in Baghdad, the capital of the [Arab] Orient, one could find nothing like it.

Long before [European] colonization, then, Black Africa had acceded to civilization. According to Ibn Batouta [a 14th century, Arab Muslim scholar], the roads in the interior of Africa were absolutely safe.³

> 'Acts of injustice are rare among them [Blacks]: of all peoples, this is the one least inclined to commit these and the sultan (Negro king) never forgives anyone who is guilty of one. Through the length and breadth of the country reigns perfect security; people can live there and travel without fear of robbery or depredation. They do not confiscate the goods of white men who die in their country; even when the value of these is immense, they do not touch them; on the contrary, they appoint trustees of the inheritance, chosen among the white men and it remains in their hands until the rightful owners come to claim it' (Ibn Batouta, Voyage au Soudan, p. 36).⁴

Words must be issued concerning traditional, East and West Afrikan nations; the torch of independent civilization would be transferred to these Black states after the destruction of ancient No. Afrikan civilizations by Caucasians. As borrowed from C.A. Diop, a premise of this text is that 1,000s of years of settled life in a warm and fertile climate engendered in Afrikans a mentality and social traits completely opposite to those of Caucasians (Europeans, Arabs, Aryans, etc.). Medieval eyewitness Ibn Battuta's assessment of the integrity of W. Afrikans is reminiscent of the ancient Greeks' observations of the Ethiopians and Egyptians: Peaceful, accepting (xenophilic) Blacks were virtually without greed, dishonesty, thievishness or criminality. Fertile and clement geography ensured virtuous characteristics among traditional (non-Islamized), East and West Afrikans and vibrant 4th-16th century economies.

Of course, Arabs were hasty to trade in the riches of East and West Afrikan economies: "Against the camel's mange [skin disease] use tar, and against poverty make a trip to the [W. Afrikan] Sudan" (Diop, Precolonial Black Africa, p. 136). The abundance of gold mines, in W. Afrika, and, previously, in ancient Ethiopia (Nubia), ensured that Black constitutional monarchs did not have to impoverish common citizens with taxes and tariffs; the White citizens of medieval Europe would not experience such a fortunate condition. More specifically, C.A. Diop discerns, from the documentation of 14th century eyewitness Al Bakri, that mineral wealth was so abundant in W. Afrika that citizens were allowed to extract all available gold dust (not chunks) from Ghanian mines.

C.A. Diop says Arab travelers of medieval W. Afrika encountered no poverty there; according to 14th century, Black Muslim scholar Mahmud Kati, the King of Ghana issued 10,000 meals nightly to citizens in the capitol city Kumbi-Kumbi.

Much of the remainder of this chapter will feature the tragic depopulation and devastation of materially-comfortable, population-dense metropolises, etc. in Afrika by Arabs and Europeans.

> Professor E. Torday points out that it was on a [Afrikan] peasantry, in many respects superior to serfs in large areas of Europe, that the slave trade fell. [European] Slavers manufactured quarrels among tribesmen and set them at each other's throats, taking care, of course, to supply them with modern weapons. Tribal life was broken up or undermined and millions [1,000,000s] of de-tribalized or decentralized Africans were let loose upon each other. The excesses of the slave trade must never be forgotten, for in them lie much of the [contemporary] horrors of the African continent.
>
> As they [European slavers] devastated an area they moved westward and southward, spreading confusion, anarchy, and ruin wherever they went. They extended the gospel of doom past the Niger [River] and by 1789, they had initiated Mozambique into their slave-raiding ideology. Traders travelled hundreds and sometimes thousands of miles from one side of the vast continent to the other without molestation, for the

stranger was always an honoured guest to the African. Tribal wars from which European pirates claimed to deliver people were mere sham-fights; it was a great battle when half a dozen men perished on a battlefield. To quote Professor Emil Torday: 'Central Africa was a territory of peace and happy civilization.'[5]

For those who require the specific details and examples of just how the advancing Black states were destroyed throughout the African continent-and want fact repeated over and over again--here then is still another example in both Angola and the Kingdom of Kongo. The strategy for destruction seldom varied, and so giving added weight to my concept of a Grand Caucasian Consensus on matters concerning non-white peoples. The aim was to provoke war between Blacks (A few old guns replacing spears seemed to be sufficient evidence that these whites were indeed saviours as well as friends), pitting the gun-armed groups against those who only had shields and spears, and thus sky-rocketing the number of captives for slavery from a few 1,000s into millions. Not only were whole villages destroyed, but entire provinces were depopulated and their formerly proud and free citizens marched off in chains, collared and joined together with heavy poles.

A partial view of the early history of Blacks ... has been presented through a summary study of a representative number of [Afrikan] states; a continent -wide view of what happened to the whole by looking at typical situations-a people forever migrating, forever on the move, forever in flight from threats to survival; ... but every decade of unsettled life, every decade of wandering over deserts, savannas and through forests--every such decade was one of retrogression, of disintegration--decades of decline, and no newly established state [e.g., Kuba; Kongo-Angola; Monomotapa; etc.] was able to reach the level of achievements of the past before it was engulfed either by the Islamic East or the Christian West. This is what we have witnessed, no matter what Black state was studies or in what region of Africa it was located.

The worst outcome from the forced migrations all over Africa in the long search for places of refuge and freedom were the endless splintering off of societies into countless little isolated states. Unity, in terms of keeping a very large group together, was impossible. Seldom could 10,000 people move en masse, not to mention 100,000--one-hundred thousand would be a small number if it was a great state that was being disorganized and destroyed. Worse still, Blacks have been so busy being 'different' through all these years that they have been unable to see that underlying all of their cultural varieties is compelling evidence that they are all members of the same race and have the same common origin.[6]

It has been documented that there was no poverty among the medieval West Afrikan empires (nation-states); on the basis of the lack of poverty alone, those nation-states could be considered great. Considering the humane distribution of resources and wealth, surely modern-day, underclass Afrikan-Americans would appreciate the superiority of traditional (non-Islamized), constitutional monarchies or theocracies in comparison to feudal (semi-slave), European governments or contemporary European-American capitalist-democracy. If a premise of this manuscript is understood--1,000s of years of nomadic life in Europe and Asia created in Caucasians instincts of extreme materialism, xenophobia, war and criminality--the Black reader will appreciate that traditional, constitutional monarchies (e.g., among the Yoruba and Akan; Cayor (Senegal); Mossi; Ghana; etc.), of 4th-

16th century, East or West Afrika, were superior to any medieval government of the Caucasian world. Only inferior, de-centralized governments existed in a Europe besieged by barbaric, Caucasian (Mongals, aryans, Norsemen, etc.) invasions, beginning at the end of Antiquity and continuing through the Early Ages (ca 700-1100 c.e.).

The Arabs deserve great credit for initiating the modern trade in Black slaves, prior to the Europeans: The 14th and 15th century enslavement and weakening of East and Central Afrikans (e.g., Mozambicans, Congolese, etc.) paved the way for their conquest by Europeans. In pursuit of precious salt mines in W. Afrika and with the aid of artillery in 1590 c.e., greedy Moroccan Arabs brutalized and burned to the ground the Songhai Empire metropolises of Djenne, Gao (the capitol), and Timbuktu. Of course, European slave-traders were ravaging first the W. Afrikan coast, while Arabs wreaked havoc in the rest of the continent. According to historian J.C. deGraft Johnson, Timbuktu was depopulated from 200,000 to a total of 15,000 Black survivors. Retribalization (isolation), which plagues Afrikan tribes to this day, was the natural result of the Arab and European destabilization of medieval and post-1500 c.e., Black civilizations.

I would ask the Black reader to recall forever the dismemberment of the Afrikan, Akan group (described in Chapter Five), as a result of Islam, and the depopulation of the cities Djenne, Gao, and Timbuktu by the Arabs; however, the Europeans would surpass the greedy Arabs in destabilizing the entire Afrikan continent. Among others, the great, Black historians C.A. Diop, J. deGraft Johnson, W. Rodney and Chancellor Williams agree that the current-day existence of splintered, retribalized (isolated), and suspicious Afrikan groups, with language barriers, is a direct result of the Arab and European disruption of Black civilization.

> 'There is no doubt that the resources and labor of Afrika have built the West. The modern slave was the foundation on which Western civilization was built.'[7] Slavery, ..., had become the very foundation upon which it [Virginia and the southern colonies of the U.S.] was established. It was the wealth accumulated from the West Indian

trade [in sugar and slaves, etc.] which more than anything else underlay the prosperity and civilization of New England and the Middle Colonies [In America].[8] [Malcolm X:] The only reason that the present generation of white Americans are in the position of economic strength is because their fathers worked our [Black] fathers for over 400 years with no pay. For over 400 years we [Blacks] worked for nothing. We were sold from plantation to plantation like you sell a horse, or a cow, or a chicken, or a bushel of wheat.

All of that money that piled up from the sale of my mother and my grandmother and my great-grandmother is what gives the present generation of [European-] Americans (the ability) to walk around the earth with their chest out; you know, like they have some kind of economic ingenuity.[9]

'European nations and nationalism, Arab nations and nationalism grew and prospered from the slave trade. Western society is the history of the modern slave trade, and Western society is a slave culture.'[10] The British Empire was 'a magnificent superstructure of American commerce and [British] naval power on an African foundation. (M. Postlewayt, The African Trade, the Great Pillar ..., 1745 a.d.)' Great banks were founded, great businesses were based on the profits of the slave system. Many of the 18th century banks established in Liverpool and Manchester, the [British] slaving metropolis and cotton capital respectively, were directly associated with the triangular trade [between Europe, Afrika, and the Americas]. The rise of banking in Glasgow was intimately connected with the triangular trade [involving Afrikan slaves].

The triangular trade [in slaves and sugar, etc.] made an enormous contribution to Britain's industrial development. The profits from this triangular [slave] trade fertilized the entire productive system of the country. Britain was accumulating great wealth from the triangular trade. The increase of consumption goods called both by that trade inevitably drew in its train the development of the productive power of the country. ... Absentee [British] planters [of W. Indies sugar-plantations using slaves] purchased land in England, where they were able to use their wealth to finance the great developments associated with the Agricultural Revolution. ... The investment of profits from the triangular [slave] trade in British industry ... supplied part of the huge outlay for the construction of vast plants to meet the needs of the new productive process and new markets.

The triangular trade [in Black slaves] thereby gave a triple stimulus to British industry. By 1750 there was hardly a trading or manufacturing town in England which was not in some way connected with the triangular or direct colonial [American] trade (J. Gee, Trade and Navigation of Great Britain Considered, 1750 a.d.). The profits obtained provided one of the main streams of that accumulation of capital in England which financed the Industrial Revolution. Some of the capital which financed the growth of the metallurgical [heavy] industries (which played an important role in the progress of the Industrial Revolution) was supplied directly by the triangular trade [in slaves and sugar, etc. between Europe, Afrika, and the Americas]. It was the capital accumulated from the West Indian trade [in slaves and sugar] that financed James Watt and the steam engine. What was characteristic of

British capitalism was typical also of capitalism in France. Gaston-Martin writes:

> There was not a single great shipowner in Nantes [France] who, between 1714 and 1789, did not buy and sell slaves; there was not one who sold only slaves; it is almost as certain that none would have become what he was if he had not sold slaves. In this lies the essential importance of the slave trade: on its success or failure depended the progress or ruin of all the others.'[11]

Only independent, Black schools will insure that Afrikan children in America learn quickly what the inimitable genius Malcolm X (al hajj Malik Shabazz) deduced: The capital accumulated from the 15th-19th century sale and exploitation of Black slaves explains the current-day, economic superiority of European-Americans. Surely the onethird of the Afrikan-American population which occupies the underclass or poverty class will appreciate their impoverished condition while considering the origin of the material wealth and goods flaunted before them by well-to-do White classes.

Given the mention of the European and European-American trade in Black slaves, I am drawn to a comparison between internal slavery in Europe and Afrika, respectively. White slaves were the economic foundation of ancient Greco-Roman culture; also, the trade in Afrikan slaves has been the foundation of modern European and EuropeanAmerican societies. It is wrong to believe that Christianity ended White slaves in Europe; C.A. Diop says, in the Early and Middle Ages (ca. 700-1500 c.e.), Europe practiced internal slavery as numerous and more despicable than that which Afrika practiced (<u>Precolonial Black Africa</u>, p. 152). A ponderous class of European serfs were in medieval, economic bondage--they were bound to land owned by feudal lords; while Karl Marx pointed to the White roundsmen as the 19th century slaves of European towns or parishes (<u>Precolonial Black Africa</u>, p. 152).

Internal Afrikan slavery resulted when one national territory took as prisoners-of-war the soldiers and freemen of another territory, due to some trade, religious, or social dispute. However, C.A. Diop cites existing medieval, Arabic documents to show that Black slaves who were not deported to the Americas, etc. experienced living conditions remarkably superior to those of white slaves in Europe. For example, in the great, traditional (non-Islamized) states of Mossi, Ghana, Cayor (Senegal), and pre-Islamized Hausa (Nigeria) and Kanem-Bornu (Lake Chad area), etc., constitutional monarchies, vastly superior to feudal European governments, allowed slaves to be represented directly among the Council of Ministers who elected the king. This slave-Minister was also the Minister of Finances; High Executioner of condemned criminals; chief of the slaves of the Crown; chief of the sacred profession of blacksmiths; and governor over a province of freemen or citizens; additionally, once chosen, no minister could be removed by the king (Diop, Precolonial Black Africa, pp. 43-5). The capacity of traditional, Afrikan constitutional-monarchies to share the power of the king with the common citizens and slaves did not have an equal among medieval European governments.

"By the time of [Islamized-empire] Mali's pre-eminence in the 13th and 14th centuries, a small amount of local slavery had come into existence, and, by the end of the 15th century, there were both chattel [sellable] slaves and 'domestic' slaves comparable to [European] feudal serfs" (W. Rodney, How Europe Underdeveloped Africa, p. 60).

According to medieval, Arabic documents, slaves of the Afrikan kings of Mali and the [Islamized] Askias of Gao [capitol city of the Songhai Empire] enjoyed complete liberty of movement. It seems obvious that the vast majority of extra-territorial Black natives captured as prisoners-of-war "... were, more, and more, sort of 'subjects' of the king. The social condition of the slaves has been clearly shown: their treatment was not inhumane, ..., as long as they remained within the area [Black Afrika];....

After the contact with Europe, the lot of Africa's slaves suddenly got worse, since it then became possible for them to be sold to persons [i.e., Europeans] who would export them, with the whole chain of well-known evils entailed in these forced [Atlantic O.] crossings" (Precolonial Black Africa, pp. 152-53, 157).

Indeed, the captive Afrikan Olaudah Equiano (renamed Gustavus Vassa) experienced the absolute horrors of a forced Atlantic Ocean crossing aboard an 18th century slave ship. Equiano witnessed cruelty and savagery by the European slavers unequaled among Black people (see <u>The Interesting Narrative of the Life of Olaudah Equiano, or Gustavus Vassa the African, written by himself</u>, 1789).

The eyewitness Equiano confirms that the life of indigenous slaves confined to Black Afrika (that is, Afrika south of the Sahara) was incomparably superior to Black slaves transported to the Americas, etc. For instance, among Equiano's Ibo tribe of W. Afrika (present-day Nigeria), there was scarcely a different between slaves (i.e., prisoners-ofwar) and the common citizens; slaves did not do more work than their masters or other members of the community! In addition, one can deduce from Olaudah Equiano's 1789 narrative that Whites inspired Afrikans to enslave other local Blacks, in order to exchange them for the goods of the invading Europeans.

> Pressures from the African population increased with widespread [European] slave hunts and raids. [Western] Historians have highlighted the role of African chiefs and kings in the slave trade; little is said about the general African opposition to the trade or about the kings and chiefs who led the fight against it. Queen Nzinga [of Ndongo-Matamba or current-day Angola] was not the only African abolitionist. The Kongolese opposing their kings were fighting both slavery and Christian Church that promoted it.[12]

> The docility of the Negro slave is a myth. The Maroons of Jamaica and the Bush Negroes of the British Guiana [So. America] were runaway slaves who had extracted treaties from the British Government and lived independently in their mountain vastness or jungle retreats. The successful slave revolt in St. Dominique [West Indies] was a landmark in the history of slavery in the New World, and after 1804, when the

independent republic of Haiti was established, every white slave-owner, in Jamaica, Cuba, or Texas, lived in dread of another Toussaint L'Ouverture [the brilliant Black who led the slave revolt in St. Dominique, Haiti].[13] The impression prevails in certain quarters that the Negro under slavery [in the Americans] was a docile being who never struck a blow in defence of his own freedom; but this is an utterly false impression. Edward D'Auvergne, in his Human Livestock, writes:

> 'The fears of the earlier [plantation] planters were justified by repeated servile insurrections. These revolts of the damned against the [European] fiends were all unsuccessful, either suppressed with hideous cruelty or nipped in the bud through the treachery generally of some soft-hearted servant who did not wish her master or mistress to be 'murdered.' Koromantees [Gold Coast Afrikans] were almost always the prime movers in these conspiracies. In 1676, according to a contemporary account published in London, their [Koromantee] ... plot [in the Americas] was frustrated and the ringleaders apprehended. Six were burnt alive.'[14]

During 400 years of deportation of Blacks in America there was true militancy in Black people because there were 156 revolts.... One hundred years ago [prior to 1864 c.e.], you had men like Nat Turner, and others, Toussaint L'Ouverture. None of them would submit to slavery.[15] There have been periods in ... history when black erupted in activities that were more clearly insurrectionary--for example, the slave conspiracies during the first third of the 19th century: Gabriel Prosser's plan to capture

Richmond, Virginia; the plantation uprisings around New Orleans led by Deslandes; Denmark Vesey's conspiracy to capture Charleston, S.C.; or the Nat Turner rebellion in Southampton County, Va. The number of blacks who participated ran into the 1,000s, ... although these efforts were usually betrayed [by weak-minded Black slaves] and always crushed ...[16] In 1811 c.e., 500 Negro men and women of the parish of St. John the Baptist, Louisiana, revolted with a slight success. But later they were beaten by the [White] militia and their heads cut off and stuck on high poles along the river and the plantations for miles.[17]

Our [Blacks'] introduction to the West is a history so filled with blood, hurt and death that it should be carefully implanted in every Black person's mind: We must not forget, again. The Aryans blatant disregard for Black life greatly weakened the Afrikan physically and psychologically:

> 'The oppressive acts consisted of cropping ears, ... On numerous occasions, the planters branded, stabbed, tarred and feathered, burned, shackled, tortured, maimed, crippled, mutilated and castrated their slaves' (J.W. Blasinggame, The Slave Community).

> '... The whites ... by subjecting us to slavery, and having murdered so many millions of us, ... strip and beat us one before the other--chain, hand-cuff and drag us about like rattle-snakes--shoot us down like wild bears, before each other's faces,....' (David Walker's Appeal, 1829).

Assimilation for those Afrikans brought to America was a slave-making process of inducing Blacks to think and act as white people with no individual or collective will. For those Afrikans who would not submit to breeding, rape, and acculturation (slave-making), etc., the answer was simple: kill them, thus making them examples.[18]

For every two million Blacks enslaved over a million died. The record [e.g., the narrative eye-witness Olaudah Equiano] indicates rather clearly that many millions preferred death to slavery.[19] It has been estimated that the slave trade swallowed up one hundred to three hundred million [300,000,000] individuals, dead or shipped to America.[20] At the end of slavery [1865 c.e.], you didn't have twenty-five million Afrikans in the Western hemisphere.[21]

The Euro-Asian trade in Afrikan slaves crippled the Black race,.... We now stand as a defeated and conquered people; therefore, more than at any time in our history we need a fighting history--a war history documenting our struggle against white domination over the past 5,000 years. To talk about whom we lost [during the Euro-Arab trade in Black slaves] speaks most to our current ... under-development. We lost the greatest independent thinkers, those who refused to be slaves and chose death for themselves and their families; we [Blacks] lost scientists, the master teachers, doctors, religious leaders, and craftsmen...[22]

Blacks are still enslaved today: all our life-sustaining institutions are controlled by Europeans (whites) and that is slavery, not oppression.[23] Black people in the U.S. are in a slave position. Essentially, we as a people have traveled from chattel slavery to the present state of neo-slavery. The [home-] land issue and Black nationalism [should] have formed the burning unanswered question for Black people in the Western hemisphere [the Americas, W. Europe, etc.]. One

> of the most obvious truths is that we have become
> accustomed to being slaves. We [Blacks in the
> U.S.] are the most comfortable slaves in the world,
> and are totally dependent upon [white people] ...
> for everything life-giving, e.g., water, food,
> clothing, housing, values, transportation,
> communications, etc.[24]

In the absence of independent, Black schools, Blacks (Afrikans) in America are left to imagine that all Afrikans watched passively as fellow Blacks were enslaved by Europeans and Arabs. However, the remaining army of greedy Moroccan Arabs, who had invaded the Islamized, W. Afrikan Songhai Empire in 1590 c.e., was finally chased from Timbuktu by the non-Islamized (?) leader Oghmor and the Afrikan masses in 1737, after 150 years of battle.[25] Only children graduates of (The Council of) Independent Black Institutions will have had the most remote chance to learn that, instead of being only docile or willing contributors to their own enslavement and European colonization (domination), Black chiefs and kings and the general Afrikan population opposed the modern slave trade. For instance, historian Chancellor Williams says King Affonso (in spite of his Portugese name) began to resist the Slave Trade and Portugese Caucasianization of the Kongo in 1512 c.e., while Queen Ann Nzinga fought the Portugese in Angola from 1623 to her death in 1663. Only Afrikan-Americans (i.e., Afrikans in America) attending independent Black Institutions (not White-controlled Negro colleges) will have the opportunity to develop an Afrikan, national-historic personality, while learning that the warrior Ashanti people fought and defeated both the British and Dutch in the Gold Coast (Ghana) for 200 years, from the 17th to the 19th century, and the So. African Zulu-king Bambaata (following the tradition of warrior-kings
Chaka and Cetewayo) fought the Dutch and British unceasingly, until his demise in 1906 c.e.

Beginning with the Foreword to this text, I have advocated that historically-aware Blacks in America arm themselves technologically to return to redevelop AFrika industrially, politically, etc. This <u>final</u> solution will appear very simple to those thousands of Afrikans across America who have had the courage, perseverance, and ingenuity to create the national system of

Independent Black Institutions. Analogically speaking, it is unwise (stupid) for a Black person to leave his (her) original identity (Mother Afrika) underdeveloped in favor of a new identify and home (European-America). Blacks will obtain the desire and urgency to return and participate in the redevelopment of their original homeland by cultivating an Afrikan, national-historic awareness, which will encompass or lead to an Afrikan worldview or frame of reference. It is from the present national system of independent Black schools (The Council of Independent Black Institutions) that Black students will develop a new Afrikan personality and frame of reference. Is it not obvious that all Afrikan (Black) parents must either create independent Black schools and institutions in their respective, present locations or relocate to one of the metropolitan centers where an independent Black school exists? Indeed, the salvation of all Afrikans (Blacks) in America rests, eventually, in their gravitating to independent Black schools (not White-controlled Negro colleges) and institutions, wherever they exist throughout America. Negroes who are not willing to relocate to independent schools or create independent, Black institutions in their respective locations represent the world's best-paid slaves and are comfortable serving the European-American socio-economic, political system.

The Black-genius Haki Madhubuti agrees with the Black multi-genius C.A. Diop: Conservatively speaking, two hundred and fifty million (250,000,000) Blacks were killed by Europeans and Arabs in their trades in African slaves. Additionally, 18th century eyewitness Olaudah Equiano (Gustavus Vassa) confirms the mental-giant Chancellor Williams' observation that millions of Blacks preferred death to enslavement; the Afrikan Equiano watched Blacks hurl themselves overboard to escape the slave ship.

> Had the evolution of Africa not been arrested by the impact of [European] Imperialism, we would undoubtedly have wide multi-national political structures today. The political evolution of Precolonial African states was going towards large spatial structures.[26] [For example,] Systematic [European] attempts to conquer the Ashanti started in 1823 a.d.... By 1873 this black [Ashanti]

nation had overrun the whole of the Gold Coast [modern-day Ghana], even forcing out the Dutch. But in [1873 c.e.] ... the Fanti, with whom [the Ashanti] King Kofi was at war, called in their allies, the British. The Ashanti fought with traditional valor, but long-distance cannon beat them,.... The English invasion had more or less disrupted the country and native tribes, who had taken to fighting among themselves, were difficult to curb. W.W. Claridge, an English writer, said:

> The destruction of the central [Ashanti] controlling authority in Kumassi and the weakness of the [British] government in declining all further responsibility and refusing to interfere for the preservation of order had caused years of civil war during which the suffering and loss of life must have been immeasurably greater than that attending the occasional wars of united Ashanti....'[27]

There were tribes in Africa before the [European] imperialist penetration, but no 'tribalism' in the modern sense. Tribalism arose from [European] colonialism, which exploited ... tribal survivals to combat the growth of [Black] national liberation movements.[28] All of the large states of 19th century Africa were multi-ethnic [i.e., multi-tribal], and their expansion was continually making anything like 'tribal' loyalty a thing of the past, by substituting in its place national and class ties. However, in all parts of the world, that substitution of national and class ties for purely ethnic ones is a lengthy historical process;.... In the first place, [European] colonialism blocked the further evolution of national solidarity, because it destroyed the particular ... African states which were principal agent for achieving the liquidation of fragmented [tribal] loyalties.

Human activity within small groups connected only by kinship relations (such as the tribe) is a very transient phase through which all the continents passed.... When it [tribalism] ceased to be transient and became institutionalized in Africa, that was because [European] colonialism interrupted African development.[29]

The formation of nationalities was retarded as a result of colonial conquest, when the [European] imperialists carved up Africa among themselves, disregarding geographical, linguistic and ethnic realities. The normal growth of the economy ... of African society was hindered and distorted. Patriarchal and feudal structures were artificially preserved.[30] European colonialism created Kwashiorkor [extreme malignant malnutrition] in Africa. ... Bourgeois propaganda has conditioned even Africans to believe that malnutrition and starvation were the natural lot of Africans from time immemorial. Oxfam [the large British charitable operation] never bothered the consciences of the people of Europe [and America] by telling them that capitalism and colonialism created starvation, suffering, and the misery of African children in the first place.[31]

... Tribalism is being superseded everywhere and must progressively die out in the consciousness of all Africans. It [tribalism] belongs therefore to a form of socio-political organization and is observable in the evolution of all human societies. Colonialization and the slave trade helped to retribalize Africa. Each ethnic [tribal] community in Africa once enjoyed a continuous territorial base. [European] Colonialism created a new and difficult situation when it drew arbitrary borders. Yet, that situation has segmented many ethnic [tribal] communities. Take the Hausas, for example. We find them split between French-speaking Niger and English-speaking Nigeria. The Yorubas have suffered a similar fate, split between Nigeria and Benin and so on. A young, dynamic leadership, animated by the purest patriotic motives and sentiments, can bring about viable and political structures anywhere in Africa. Only the most patriotic of sentiments and the most unselfish of political behaviors can save Africa in this sense.[32]

Lo and behold, based upon the learned analyses of Black scholars quoted above, the reader can understand that the Slave Trade and European colonization and imperialization (domination) have interrupted Afrikan social and economic development, retribalized Afrika, and blocked the evolution of national solidarity and multi-national, political structures in Afrika. The military, political and economic domination of Afrikans by Europeans has prevented the natural evolution of a United States of Afrika. The reader should understand that the political organization of traditional, medieval (precolonial) constitutional-monarchies in Black Afrika was superior to contemporary European governments. The political constitutions of non-Islamized Mossi (W. Afrika) and Cayor (Senegal), etc., were in effect for nearly 2,000 years before the interference of European military colonialism (Diop, Precolonial Black Africa, p. 47, 99-100.

On the other hand, after the 4th century breakup of the Roman Empire and due to barbaric, medievalists (ca. 700-1500 c.e.) invasions, Europeans were unable to create sophisticated, centralized governments.

Given the absence of independent, Black schools and the European de-culturalization of Blacks (Africans) in America, including the propagation of Negrophobic myths and stereotypes such as Ham, the Sambo, Pickaninny, Mammy, Tarzan and Jane (although only 5-10% of Afrika is jungle), etc., it is little wonder that Afrikan-Americans denounce openly their Afrikan heritage and indicate their unwillingness to consider returning to redevelop their original homeland. As an example of the debasement and desensitization of Afrikan-Americans to their original homeland/culture, the reader should examine the degrading remarks of Colorado beer-magnate William K. Coors. As quoted by the <u>Rocky</u> <u>Mountain News</u> (T. Schilling, "Coors Calls Blacks 'Intellectual' Inferiors," 24 March 1984, p. 64) and appearing before 150 Black and Hispanic business owners, William Coors said the following:

> 'They [i.e., indigenous Afrikans in Black-governed Afrika] lack the intellectual capacity to succeed [economically], and it's taking them down the tubes. ... One of the best things they (slave traders) did for you [Afrikan-Americans] is to drag your ancestors over here in chains.' The outspoken chairman and chief executive officer of the Adolph Coors Co. said if American blacks visited the African countries from which their ancestors were taken by [European] slave traders, they would be glad they were living in a country with a free-enterprise system, 'a land of opportunity.'

William Coors and his ignorant remarks on Afrikan culture are the products of a most -privileged, multi-millionaire White family; Blacks can only shudder to think what backwards misconceptions average White people entertain about Afrikans and Afrikan high-culture. William Coors' Negrophobic remarks are even more disgusting in light of their afore-quoted historian W. Rodney: The slave trade, colonialism, and capitalism of Europeans and European-Americans is responsible for initially for the current starvation, suffering, and misery of Afrikan people. The Coors statements were deemed so outrageous that the Coors beer empire was coerced into signing a multi-year, multimillion dollar trade agreement with the National Association for the Advancement of Colored People (N.A.A.C.P.) in order to end a national boycott of Coors Co. product.

All indigenous Black Afrikans (Afrikans living south of the Sahara) are not aware that they will always be under attack from Western, multi-intelligence agencies, which seeks to control the social and political economies of Black Afrikan states.

Philip Agee, a twelve-year, CIA (U.S. Central Intelligence Agency), secret-operations officer, whose career ended in 1969, acknowledges that the CIA plotted and participated in the overthrow of the Black governments of Zaire (formerly the Congo) and Ghana (see P. Agee, Inside the Company: CIA Diary, 1975, pp. vii-ix). Surely Black people must see any hope of Afrikan progress diminish when they recall that the American government participated in the exile of Kwame Nkrumah (Ghana) and murder of Patrice Lumumba (the Congo)--two independent-minded, Black Afrikan leaders. More recently, the capitalist, U.S. government has provided military arms and $15 million per year to UNITA (Union for the Total Independence of Angola) rebels to attack the Marxist (?), Cuban-supported, Black Afrikan government of Angola (see J. Brooke, "CIA Said to Send Weapons Via Zaire to Angola Rebels," The New York Times, 2-1-87, Sect. 1).

> Much of the confusion in Afrika stems from its centuries of white supremacy, colonialism, and imperialism imposed on its people from outside. The United States' connection to Afrika currently replaces that of her mother Europe. Lenin focused on the modern scramble for Afrika as the explanation for the origin of World War I. In his Imperialism: The Highest Stage of Capitalism (1916) he [V.I. Lenin] developed the thesis that the quest for Arikan territory by the European (capitalist) powers inevitably led to the First World War.
>
> The worldwide-Imperialist stranglehold that the [U.S.] State Department and the U.S. Corporate structure have over much of the world is not divinely endowed and must be attacked.[33] Colonialism increased the dependence of Africa on Europe in terms of the numbers of persons brought into the money economy and in terms of the number of aspects of socio-economic life in Africa which derived their existence from the connection with the [European] metropole.[34]

Africa has produced only one [Julius] Nyerere [of Tanzania] and maintained him in power, while we [Black Afrikans] have murdered Lumumba and have locked up or exiled leaders like ... Nkrumah in response to the wishes of [European and European-American] imperialists--our donor, our money-lenders, our patrons, our master, our trading partners. It is difficult to imagine, apart from one or two honorable exceptions, any of the present [Afrikan] leaders who is capable of standing up for the genuine rights of his people, knowing that these rights are of necessity directly opposed to the interests of [Caucasian] imperialism.[35]

We [Black Afrikans] are still not free, however, even after this loosening of [European colonial] bonds. We will never be allowed to select a political and social regime different from those of the [capitalist] Western world without running the risk of having to fight or seeing ourselves overthrown by intrigues, making use of local parties of Western allegiance. This is the last camouflaged line of retreat for the batteries of the imperialist West, alleging that its own economic fate and 'civilization as we know it' depend on retaining control of Africa. The new [European and American] tactic rather consists in trying to direct Black African national liberation movements, to channel them toward non-socialistic forms, of the so-called Western type. If this goal were reached, ... Black Africa would be ... SouthAmericanized. It would be made up of a proliferation of little dictator-ridden countries without organic [cultural, racial] ties one to another, ephemeral, afflicted with chronic weakness, governed by terror with the help of outside police forces, but under the economic domination by foreign countries, pulling strings through the mere presence of an [foreign] embassy. This was the case in Guatemala [Central America], where ...: A foreign business firm, the Fruit Co. (U.S.), overthrew the local government and replaced it with another more amenable to the company's aims, working in conjunction with the American embassy (and, as we now know, the CIA), thus proving the emptiness of the so-called independence of such a state. (Since these lines were first written [1960 c.e] this process of South-Americanization has indeed begun in Black Africa. The phenomenon has become generalized: Civilian [Black Afrikan] governments are today the exception.)[36]

... There is very little time left before our [Black Afrikan] economies become permanently distorted and probably too damaged for any meaningful reconstruction in the future. It is clear, foreign [European and American] investment is 'the cause,' and not a solution to our [Black Afrikan] economic backwardness. The more we [Black Afrikans] invest in export branches in order to capture the 'world market' ... the less effective our development effort. [37]

Chapter 7

A Comparison of Political and Socio-Economic Structures in Europe and Precolonial Black Afrika.
(To my psychological mentor Cheikh Diop)

> African collectivism, the moral and material security it assured every individual, ... made useless, if not superfluous, the accumulation of excessive wealth; even the riches of the king do not seem huge by modern standards.[1] In Europe, individualism led to entrepreneurship and adventurism of the type which spearheaded Europe's conquest of the rest of the world.[2] African collectivism and European individualism grow out of the material conditions of existence.[3] The rigors of seasonal climate and the necessity of every moving onwards in search of game did not encourage communal life (from the 8th millennium before the Christian
> Era, in Europe from England to the Urals [mountains bordering the
> U.S.S.R.]), and until after the beginning of the Christian Era and
> [Caucasian] hunters of the north continued to shelter themselves in caves or thickets, or at best to erect crude huts of saplings founded on a circle of stones and roofed with thatch or skins. In the south, however, in ... Africa, thee amelioration of climate which accompanied the Pluvial Period created more favorable living conditions. About the fifth millennium b.c., ... branches of the human stock ... developed a communal life based on agriculture.[4]

It has already been seen that, in passing from South [Afrika] to North [Europe], geography, climate and the conditions of existence effectively reversed the moral values, which become opposed to each other like the two poles: every defect here is a virtue there. It is by remembering the criteria of the war-like northern morality particularly of the Aryan Germans, a morality necessitated by the conditions of life, that one can understand the slow formation, through contact with antagonistic outside [Afrikan] influences, of a feeling of moral unease terminating in the idea of guilt among some of them, of sin among others, both specifically Northern [Caucasian] sentiments, although collective. Nietzche [the famed German philosopher] was therefore right in making criminality and sin a constitutional component of the Aryan conscience.... The xenophobia of the Northern [i.e., European] countries, in contrast to the xenophilia of [Black, Afrikan] countries with a matriarchal regime was such that at the time of Herodotus, in the 5th century [b.c.e.], only a [1] soothsayer [Homer?] had as yet acquired Athenian [Greek] nationality, while in Egypt, according to M. Fontanes [Les Egyptes, p. 169] from the time of the 12th dynasty [ca. 2100 b.c.e.], Black, White and Yellow men had already been admitted to live as equal citizens.

In conclusion, the Meridional cradle confined to the African continent in particular, is characterized by the matriarchal family, the creation of the territorial state, in contrast to the Aryan [e.g., Greece, Rome, etc.] citystate, the emancipation of women in domestic life, xenophilia, cosmopolitanism, a sort of social collectivism having as corollary a tranquility going as far as unconcern for tomorrow, a material solidarity of right for each individual, which makes moral or

> material misery unknown to the present day [1954 c.e.]; there are people living in poverty, but no one feels alone and no one is in distress. In the moral domain, in [the Afrikan, Southern cradle] shows an ideal of peace, of justice, of goodness and an optimism....
>
> The Northern cradle [Europe], ..., is characterized by the patriarchal family,.... Individualism, moral and material solitude, a disgust for existence, ..., are all attributes of this cradle. An ideal of war, violence, crime and conquests, inherited from nomadic life, with as a consequence, a feeling of guilt and of original sin, ..., is the special attribute of this cradle.[5]

Similar to the rest of this manuscript, this chapter intends especially to draw into sharp focus the irreconcilable differences between Black (Afrikan) and Caucasian (European, Arab, etc.) cultures, respectively. Being as clear as possible, the originator of the Two Cradle Theory C.A. Diop states that respective Afrikan and European societies are as opposite as the two magnetic poles; accordingly, Blacks are innately xenophilic, socially-collective, cosmopolitan, peaceful, good, just, and optimistic, while Caucasians are innately xenophobic, extremely individualistic, acutely materialistic, immoral, violent, warlike, criminal, and avaricious. Interestingly, the White biologist Homer Smith's description, of the respective separate geographical regions which nurtured Europeans and Afrikans for 1,000s of years, support historian-physicist Diop's Two Cradle Theory: An inclement, European climate created individualistic, nomadic life among Caucasians, while a mild, Afrikan climate fostered collective, agrarian life among Blacks.

If the historical documentations and analyses of this text are recognized as valid, Blacks in America and the diaspora are faced with the decision to resolve permanently the impossibility of maintaining a viable Afrikan culture within Caucasian (EuropeanAmerican, etc.) society.

Given that the innate, destructive characteristics of Caucasians have compelled them to destroy Afrikan culture and people for over 4,000 years, historically-conscious Black people in the diaspora are forced to seek their separation from Caucasian society to insure Black development. To effect the redevelopment and maintenance of their originallywholesome culture and values, technologically-prepared Blacks in the diaspora must work to repatriate themselves. If any Black reader of this manuscript should possess a better and more permanent solution to the Afrikan dilemma in the U.S. diaspora, he or she has the obvious responsibility to inform the rest of the race!

> Since northern Europe is such a resourceless area they [Europeans] have always traveled south to 'dispute with the Africans' the resources of their own country.[6] Our [Western] economic attitudes are rooted in the poverty, inequality and economic peril of the past. These ideas were the products of a world in which poverty had always been [European] man's normal lot, and any other state was in degree unimaginable. This poverty was the unedifying mortification of the flesh--from hunger, sickness and cold. Those who might be freed temporarily from such burden could not know when it would strike again, for at best hunger yielded only perilously to privation.

> Western man has escaped for the moment poverty which was for so long his all-embracing fate. As with individuals so with nations. And the experience of [Western] nations with well-being is exceedingly brief. In the [European] world that had for so long been so poor, nothing was so important as to win an increase in wealth. Many suffered and many were destroyed under the harsh and unpredictable rule of competition and the market. This was not a compassionate world.[7]

> In contrast, in Africa the individual always felt dependent upon the state and socially speaking upon his peers within community life. In Africa, there always existed a reciprocal invasion of

consciences and individual liberties. In other words, each one felt that he had material [i.e., economic] and moral rights upon the personalities of other and that they reciprocally had rights on him. This held throughout all [Black Afrikan] political regimes. We shall see that it was otherwise in India for pariahs and for the [Greek and Roman] plebians of antiquity, where the [Caucasian] religious systems stipulated the impurity of these inferior classes.

Giving a divine character property is an Aryan [Caucasian] custom: in Rome, Greece, and India it led to the isolation from society of an entire category of individuals who had no family, neither hearth nor home, and no right of ownership. They would everywhere constitute the class of the wretched,.... In the [East Indian] "Laws of Manu" one can follow a meticulous description of objects that might be possessed by such and such a class and, above all, those objects the possession of which was forbidden to the lowest class and its crossbreeds. This consciousness of material interest, this exclusivism in the domain of possessions were the ideas added by Aryans to the caste system. Aryans meant to effect an economic classification of society, in India as well as in Rome and Greece,....

We must stress that this class [of 'untouchables' in India, of thetes in Greece, and of plebians in Rome] was totally absent from the unaltered southern [i.e., Black Afrikan] systems in which religious prohibitions might isolate a social category (e.g., the swineherds of Egypt),.... That is one of the fundamental differences between the African and Aryan conceptions. The swineherds of Egypt could absolutely acquire wealth in the same manner as others. They were not forbidden the possession of any goods. All traditional prohibitions of the rest of Black Africa were of the same nature and never affected material goods. On the contrary, we can unquestionably affirm that in every such instance the possibilities of material gain on the part of subjects of the category [caste] concerned were increased by a kind of sentiment of immanent justice, a kind of compensatory spirit inherent in the Black African society, for not only can they retain all their belongings, but they can increase their possessions by 'asking' for some of the others.[8]

In [ancient and medieval or precolonial] Africa, there were few slaves. In Africa, communal societies were introduced to the concept of owning alien human beings when they took captives in war. But very rapidly captives or their offspring became ordinary members of the society, because there was no scope for the perpetual exploitation of man by man in a context that was neither feudal nor capitalist. The sequence of modes of production [e.g., slavery and capitalism] noted in Europe were not reproduced in Africa. Nor was there a mode of production which was the replica of European feudalism. Feudalism involved great inequality in the distribution of land and social products.[9]

In antiquity, the vast majority of the thousands [1,000s] of slaves was white, not black.[10] Slavery as a dominant mode of production existed in Europe only.[11] Slavery was an [European] economic institution of the first importance. It had been the basis of the Greek economy and had built up the Roman Empire. It [slavery] produced the cotton to serve as a base for modern [European] capitalism. It made the American South and Caribbean Islands. Seen in historical perspective, slavery forms a part of that general picture of the

> harsh treatment of the underprivileged classes, the unsympathetic poor laws and feudal laws, and the indifference with which the rising [European] capitalist class was 'beginning to reckon prosperity in terms of pounds sterling, and ... becoming used to the idea of sacrificing human life to the deity of increased production.'[12]

First things first. In the documentation that opened this chapter, I quoted the great Black historian W. Rodney: Extreme individualism created an adventurism and so-called entrepreneurship which led to the Europeans' conquest of the world. I would be remiss if I did not add immediately that climate-induced individualism, which fostered economic exploitation and desperate adventurism, was accompanied by gunpowder and firearms which aided the European conquest of the planet. I must concur with the sentiment of Malcolm X (al hajj Malik Shabazz) that it required no ingenuity of Europeans to follow military domination in Afrika with economic exploitation and entrepreneurship.

It is worth noting that in Antiquity only Egyptian priests possessed the knowledge of gunpowder which they used during religious ceremonies (Diop, The African Origin of Civilization, p. 24). A peaceful, loving and just mentality would prevent precolonial Black Afrikans from attempting to utilize gunpowder and weapons to conquer and economically control Europeans; obviously, a greedy, criminal and warlike mentality has conditioned Caucasians to do otherwise. The Black reader must understand that my literary endeavor has not been to create a "safe" or perfectly impartial text. As I have understood and interpreted the vast research of Afrikan scholars and my own experiences, the destructive characteristics of Caucasians compel them to victimize, control, and destroy Blacks worldwide.

The same harsh and barren European geo-climate that was responsible for instilling the traits of extreme individualism and xenophobia (fear of strangers) within Caucasians was responsible also for the poverty which white economist J. Kenneth Galbreath says Europeans suffered from antiquity onward.

The coldness and scarcity of the European terrain explains the warlike compulsion of Whites to invade continuously Black Afrikan civilizations while establishing economically exploitative systems — slavery, feudalism, and capitalism — on European soil itself. The impoverished, relatively barren European environment, in which survival was uncertain, insured the imbedding of hoarding, violent, and criminal traits in Caucasians and their creation of economic systems which would be characterized by the gross inequality of wealth, land, and goods, between social classes.

Speaking of criminality, the reader should recall the ancient Greeks' (e.g., Homer, Diodorus Siculus, Aelian, Diodorus "Perigetes", Stobaeus, etc.) and medieval scholar Ibn Battuta's characterizations of Blacks as absolutely just and virtuous. Given that precolonial Afrikans were known as completely honest, it should surprise the reader that, as of 1972 c.e. as reported by sociologist Robt. Staples, Afrikan-American males constituted 42% of the U.S. jail population. Perhaps that fact is not so puzzling when one considers Afrikan-Americans have had almost 400 years to acquire criminal habits from the master-crook EuropeanAmericans who stole America from the Indians. Given the acutely materialistic and economically exploitative example of European-American capitalists accustomed to sacrificing human life for profit, is it any wonder that perverted, entrepreneurial drug-dealers have developed among Afrikan-Americans in inner cities?

A prosperous and accommodating geo-environment was primarily responsible for imbedding within precolonial Afrikans a sentiment of immanent material (economic) and moral justice. On the other hand, Whites have always attempted to organize their societies according to a division of goods and objects favoring upper classes over lower classes. C.A. Diop's analysis of the East Indian "Laws of Manu" illustrates that Aryans utilized a precise procedure to distribute material goods among the upper classes while restricting possessions among lower classes. Caucasians would work with the same vigor to maintain an economic division or classification of society in Greco-Roman and feudal and capitalist European societies.

Nurtured by an inclement and impoverished European environment for thousands of years, Caucasians were instilled with an acutely materialistic and individualistic instinct to secure one's own survival and existence only. The masses of Blacks (Afrikans) in America have yet to consider all the social and psychological problems of adapting themselves to an exploitative, capitalist economy derived from the extremely individualistic and acutely materialist instincts of European-Americans.

> Afrika is the richest continent in the world. Afrika has in its possession an abundance of all the world's 55 most important minerals. The majority of the world's gold, petroleum, diamonds, and iron ore are exported form Afrika.[13] Africa is geographically compact and in terms of natural resources potentially the richest continent in the world.[14]

> It seems that the wealth of the [Afrikan] continent always made it unnecessary for its inhabitants to risk the dangers of the high seas or the great international routes for commercial purposes. Likewise, in ancient times, the Ethiopians the Egyptians virtually never left their homelands. Egypt experienced a peasants' and slaves revolt toward the close of the Middle Kingdom, the sort common to Western [European] history ever since the Middle Ages--none of which was ever successful. In precolonial Africa, the periods of dearth were rather exceptional and ephemeral, and the general abundance of economic resources and the legendary, extraordinary wealth of the continent in fact foreclosed the birth and growth of any revolutionary spirit in the African consciousness.

Africa is characterized by abundance. Travelers of the precolonial era encountered no poverty there; according to the Tarikh el Fettach [written by Black, medieval scholar Mahmud Kati], the emperor of Ghana daily treated the people of his capital to 10,000 meals. The emperor, his heir apparent, and the notables all literally dripped with gold. So. Africa was distinguished in the world for its legendary wealth which led Arabs to say:

'Against the camel's mange use tar, and against poverty make a trip to the

Sudan. The Tarikh es Sudan [written by Black, medieval scholar Abderrahman es-Sadi] stressed how exceptional poverty was in Black Africa when describing that caused by the [16th-17th century] Moroccan occupation of Timbuktu.

The principal source of revenue for the sovereigns of Black Africa, from antiquity to modern times was gold extracted from mines. This gold, which was always abundant during the history of the African states, was the currency essential to international trade. It contributed powerfully to the economic prosperity of the country; it quite certainly meant the sovereigns did not have to overwhelm their respective peoples with taxes and tariffs.

In order to grasp the distinction between the economic conditions, the monetary situations of the lower classes in Medieval Europe and Black Africa, we would have to imagine the [European] king and feudal lords, in 1067 a.d., allowing the serfs and peasants the right to accumulate wealth equivalent to that of this African gold dust from the natural resources of their own countries. It is therefore, most important to bear in mind this economic factor in explaining the peculiar aspect of Africa's sociopolitical evolution.[15]

African communal societies had differences such as age-grades and differences between ordinary members and religious leaders such rainmakers. The concept of class as a motive force in social development had not yet come about [in Black Afrika]. Under communalism every African was assured of a sufficient land to meet his own needs by virtue of being a member of a family or community.[16] The political maturity of the African masses may to some extent be traced to the economic and social patterns of traditional times. Under communalism all the land and means of production belonged to the community. There was people's ownership. Labor was the need and habit of all. When a certain piece of land was allocated to an individual for his personal use [under traditional, Afrikan communalism], he was not free to do with it as he liked since it still belonged to the community. Chiefs were strictly controlled by counselors and were removable.[17]

The land in Africa does not belong to the [Black] conquerors; the mind of nobles is not concerned with the possession of great landed estates to be cultivated by serfs bound to the soil. Earth is a divinity: it would be sacrilege actually to appropriate any part of it. Even during the Islamic period, i.e., up to the present day, this religious concept obscurely influences the consciousness of all Africans and it has contributed historically toward stopping or restraining tendencies to form a feudal system. This metaphysics, far from constituting a minor fact in African historical sociology, was a predominant trait. If scientific explanation ignores it, all that it will grasp will be lifeless, external forms with no apparent logical connection.

Whereas during the Middle Ages the entire [European] feudal system was to be based on possession of the land through progressive despoiling of the protected [White] inhabitants-- creating the landed nobility--neither king nor lord in Black Africa every truly felt he possessed the land. Land possession there never polarized the consciousness of political power. We have seen the religious [metaphysical] factors that opposed this. The African peasant's situation and therefore diametrically opposed to that of the [European] serf bound to the soil and belonging, along with the land that he cultivated, to a lord and master.

The conditions under which ... plots of land [in Black Africa were granted] were in no way comparable to those in force during [European] feudal times: they could never result in the loss of liberty for a non-slave. Under the worst of them [conditions], they called for an annual rental guaranteed by verbal agreement, cancellable at the end of each season. Even the poor worker, the <u>navetane</u>, who possessed only the strength of his own arms, could not be reduced to slavery. In the morning he worked for the Laman, and in the afternoon for himself, on the same plot granted to him.

The African king, however powerful, was easily persuaded that the soil did not belong to him; this especially applicable to emigrant kings: they easily accepted the sacred authority of the original occupants, even if the latter were presently without any material power. The sale of land, properly speaking, seems to have been unknown in traditional precolonial Africa. In truth, the problem of land ownership appears never to have existed in Africa. Instead of land having constituted a wealth beyond the reach of certain social categories, it was within everyone's grasp,

> with no need to forfeit one's freedom, like the [European] serf bound to the soil, in order to make use of it, to 'possess' it. The slave had his own patch of ground; the stranger who just this morning came to the village would also get his.
>
> Expropriation of the sort seen in 16th century Europe was unthinkable in the history of precolonial Africa. Perhaps, it was the vast expanse of arable lands that shielded Africa from this social problem. So. Africa never had the rural capitalist who was the farm owner acting as the intermediary between the true owner of the soil and the expropriated agricultural wageearner.[18]

I can only hope that the preceding section of documentation gave the Black reader a small glimpse of the cultural environment Afrikans in the diaspora have lost. Indeed, the so-called Afrikan-America has been stripped, by his European-American masters, of all memory of the wealth of precolonial, Afrikan cultural institutions and minerals. In accordance with hearing Whites tell Blacks they should be thankful to reside in America, it is not uncommon today to hear brainwashed Afrikan-Americans stating emphatically that they would not consider returning to their Afrikan homeland. Minds filled already with negative images from Tarzan and Jane and the "Dark Continent" racial stereotypes, Blacks (Afrikans) in the U.S. have also to suffer the television and media images of Black Afrikan starvation and border-induced tribal conflicts, without knowing that, at its origin, the source of B. Afrikan turmoil and chaos is European interference. More specifically, Caucasian greed and Black xenophilia, which allowed Europeans easier access to Black Afrika, are the precursors to present-day Black Afrikan suffering and turmoil.

For what it's worth then, extreme Caucasian individualism, materialism and greed, and Black xenophilia are the sources of woe for Afrikan people worldwide. For example, even nearly 400 years of physical, psychological, and economic European-American domination have not stemmed the xenophilic acceptance of Whites by AfrikanAmericans. Of course, without the benefit of Independent Black Institutions and Schools to instill a Pan-Afrikan, national-historic consciousness, Blacks will never be cognizant of their past or potential, future Afrikan wealth and greatness. Without Independent Black Schools to teach of an Afrikan, national-historic personality, Blacks (Afrikans) in America will never understand how thoroughly Arab and European military and economic (capitalist) domination have thwarted the socio-political and economic development of all Afrikans.

How important are Independent Black Schools (i.e., The Council of Independent Black Institutions)? Participation in the national alliance of independent Black schools represents a first step toward our mental and physical separation and independence from European-America. Consequently, no Afrikan-American child should be enrolled in an integrated school environment! With respect to the long-range liberation of the entire race, Afrikan-Americans are engaged in rather inconsequential acts if they are not participating in building and maintaining independent Black (Pan-Afrikan) institutions. On a daily basis, only Afrikancentric teachers in Independent Black Schools can restore in Blacks an Afrikan, national-historic memory. The following is a brief amount of the knowledge comparing Afrikan and European cultures that Afrikancentric, Black school teachers can disseminate.

Beginning with the Nile Valley cradle, an abundantly rich and accommodating Afrikan geography created in Black citizens and monarchs (theocrats) alike a profound sense of justice and collective sociality. Average, medieval Black-Afrikan citizens were allowed to gather liberally their country's mineral riches (gold) by the kings--mentality and practice unheard of among feudal kings and lords in Europe. Metaphysical--based sociality and innately collectivist instincts, among both the nobility and common people, insured every Black Afrikan citizen of the right to occupy and cultivate land. However, feudal and capitalist, European concepts and problems of land ownership and sale did not take root in traditional, pre-European (pre-1870 c.e.) Black Afrika. Acting according to an established constitution and embodying the traits of collective and metaphysical-based sociality, traditional (non-Islamized), precolonial, Black Afrikan kings shared power willingly with officials representing each and every segment of society: C.A. Diop says no such equivalent could be found among the kings and governments of medieval Europe (Precolonial Black Afrika, pp. 43-5).

Only irreversibly brainwashed Afrikan-Americans will continue to accept the indoctrination of a corrupt, European-American capitalist-democracy, instead of acting upon the disrupted legacy of just and socially egalitarian, Black Afrikan socio-political institutions to effect positive change in their original homeland. Otherwise, AfrikanAmericans represent the world's best paid neo-slaves and are satisfied with the sociopolitical and economic crumbs from the European-American's table.

> The Empire of Ghana antedated by 500 years that of Charlemagne [a 9th century, Frankish ruler in Europe]. From the dismemberment of the Roman Empire in the 4th century until that date [the 9th century], Europe was nothing but chaos, with no organization comparable to that of the African Empire. With Charlemagne commenced the first [European] effort at centralization; but one can say without exaggeration that throughout the Middle Ages, Europe never found a form of political organization superior to that of the African states. The administrative centralization of Pharonic Egypt, with its nomes, might be brought up. Each provincial governor in Black Africa was an image of the king, with his own small court. All the necessary elements were apparently present to give rise to feudalism. So we can ask ourselves why, up to their disappearance on contact with the West [i.e., Europe], African empires did not evolve into a political feudalism through the progressive emancipation of these provincial governors. Yet, among the Mossi, once a governor was appointed, holding the rank of Minister, the King who had to designated him according to tradition could not dismiss him. We can cite ... explanations for this cohesion which was so remarkable. One of the explanations is of a

religious nature. It seems beyond doubt that, in traditional monarchies, such as the Udai in eastern Chad, the constitution was lived up to by all people. Those in charge had a religious notion of their functions, which prevented them from taking advantage of internal weaknesses in the political organization.[19]

In precolonial Africa, under the conditions of communalism, slavery and [pre-] feudalism there were embryonic class cleavages.[20] The caste system which governs African society conserves its structure and sets itself against internal upheaval. It is indispensable to insist at the outset on the specificity of the caste system. Its originality rests in the fact that the dynamic elements of society, whose discontent could have given rise to transformations, are satisfied with their social condition and do not seek to change it: a man, said to be an inferior caste, would categorically refuse to enter a so-called higher caste [occupation] if material interests alone were at stake; contrary to the [capitalist] proletarian who would willingly take the place of the employer. Society is divided into slaves and free men. In Senegal, the free men are the gor, composed of <u>ger</u> and of <u>neno</u>. The <u>ger</u> form the so-called "higher" caste. They cannot exploit, for material ends, the members of inferior castes, without themselves losing caste in the eyes of the people; they are, on the contrary, supposed to assist them in every way: even if they are less wealthy they must deprive themselves if a man of "lower" caste applies to them. In exchange the latter owe them moral respect.

The originality of this [Afrikan caste of classificatory] system arises from the fact that the manual worker instead of being cheated out of the fruit of his labour — as the [European] artisan or serf of the Middle Ages, or to a lesser extent the modern [capitalist] workman — can, on the contrary, increase it, by adding to it goods given by the nobleman. Consequently, if there were to be a social revolution, it would be accomplished from above and not below. but there is something better: the members of all the castes, including the slaves, are closely associated with authority; which leads to constitutional monarchies, governed by councils of ministers where all the authentic representatives of the people appear. it will be understood that there has never been, in [precolonial, i.e., pre-1870 c.e.] Africa, a revolution against the [political] regime, but only against those who administered it badly, that is to say, unworthy princes.

Appointments to various offices, in the traditional kingdoms, entailed the payment of a customary fee, not however, necessarily to the king. Thus, among the Mossi, ... once again we see this aspect of African social structure, this aspect of the caste system: material wealth often bypassed the chiefs and notables to pass into the hands of men of the castes, skilled workers. No comparison with the [European] feudal system in which the lord kept everything. For every [Black Afrikan] caste, inconveniences and advantages, transference of rights and compensation, all balanced each other. Whatever our present attitude toward this metaphysics of social positions, this ontology, for more than 2,000 years it ruled in an absolute manner the minds and consciences of our [Black Afrikan] ancestors: it explains, to a certain extent, their failure or success when confronted with the tasks of civilization. This is why it cannot be too minor a factor in the historical explanation; we cannot fail to consider it.[21]

> In general, at the opening of the colonial period [roughly the mid-19th century], the peoples of Africa were passing through the higher stage of communalism characterized by the disintegration of [tribal] democracy and the emergence of [pre-]feudal relationships, hereditary tribal chieftaincies and monarchial systems.[22] In the precolonial period, the entire continent was indeed covered by monarchies and empires. No spot where man lived, even in the virgin forest, escaped monarchic authority. This judgement is applicable to all of Black Africa, to different degrees.
>
> The deeper reflexes of the present-day African are more closely tied to a monarchic regime than to a republican one. Rich or poor, peasant or urbanite, all dream of being a small or great lord rather than a small or great bourgeois. The quality of their gestures and attitudes, their manner of seeing things, whatever their caste [occupation], is lordly and aristocratic in contrast to bourgeois 'pettiness.' There is still one revolution's distance between the African and Western [European] consciences, in terms of instinctive behavior. Western colonization, even when republican, could not change these facts.
>
> Africans thus never experienced a lay [non-religious] republic, even though the regimes were almost everywhere democratic, with a balance of powers. But the African was an aristocratic collectivist: .... In the light of his politico-social life, his solidarity was not a lordly one; despite that, he was loath to share; the reflexes of accumulation of material wealth remained very slight in him. Consequently, his materialistic habits rather favored a socialistic evolution.[23]

This particular narrative should prove the last for the major body of this text. As such, it should help bring to a rather conclusive end this chapter comparing Afrikan and European socio-political institutions. Consequently, I should re-mention the precolonial (pre-European) Afrikan and European cultural institutions through which social, political and economic rights are transmitted--matriarchy and patriarchy, respectively. Patriarchy, or patrilineal succession, ensures the domination of females by males in Caucasian societies; it transmitted social, political and material rights through White males only. To restate information from Chapters Two and Three, Caucasian females have held a devalued, inferior, dehumanized and deprived position in their societies since Antiquity. As taken from Diop's The African Origin of Civilization, p. 286, witness the comment of 2nd century b.c.e., Roman-statesman Cato:

> 'Our ancestors did not allow women to handle any business, even domestic, without special authorization. They never failed to keep women dependent on their fathers, brothers or husbands. List all the legislation by which our ancestors tried to curb women's independence and keep them submissive to their husbands; then see, despite all these legal obstacles, how much trouble we have in restricting them to their duties' (Livy, Histoire romaine, Book 34: "Cato's speech on maintaining the Oppia Law against the luxury of women," 195 B.C.).

On the contrary, since antiquity in traditional (non-Islamized) Black Afrika, " . . . The woman enjoyed a liberty equal to that of a man, had a legal individuality and could occupy any function" (Diop, The Cultural Unity of Black Africa, pp. 139-40). Black Afrikan matriarchy, or matrilineal succession, is defined by the transmission of social, political, and economic rights through the female. Since Antiquity in traditional Afrikan cultures, Black women have held a privileged and highly honored and respected position. In pre-European Afrika, female political-assemblies were established always with power equal to that of male, legislative assemblies (e.g., among the W. Afrikan Yoruba and Dahomeans –See Diop, Black Africa, pp. 33-4).

One intent of this manuscript has been to describe the irreconcilable psychological and instinctual differences between Afrikans and Europeans — imbedded over thousands of years by opposite physical environments. It has been my intent also that the

Black reader see how the conceptual and behavioral differences of Blacks and Caucasians resulted in completely opposite Black Afrikan and European social, political and economic institutions, respectively. For instance, in precolonial (pre-European or pre1830 c.e.), Black Afrikan, constitutional (representative) monarchies, certain administrative fees and material wealth bypassed the chiefs and nobles and went directly to the skilled workers (castes). Whereas in medieval, 8th—15th century c.e. Europe, the feudal lords kept all administrative fees — along with levies, taxes, etc. — while owning and controlling the land along with the multitude of serf-slaves bound to the soil. It was a fertile and accommodating physical environment that created and nurtured in Black Afrikans a collectively social behavior that blocked the development of feudal (i.e., landowning) concepts. In non-Islamized and pre-European Afrika, no individual owned the land, including kings, chiefs or nobles. The metaphysical (ontological, spiritual) consciousness of Black Afrikans was thus — "Earth is a divinity: it would be sacrilege actually to appropriate any part of it. It only lends itself to our agricultural activity, in order to make human life possible" (Diop, Precolonial Black Africa, p. 11). Additionally it was the morality of pre-European government officials, induced by religious (metaphysical, spiritual, etc.) notions, that supported the stability of Black Afrikan, constitutional (representative) monarchies.

Since Chapter Four, the words "clan" or "caste" have been utilized in this text. The two words/ideas can be identical in meaning, as well as identical in religious, anthropological, and ontological significance. In summary, the ontological (metaphysical) and moral significance of caste meant that a Black Afrikan, "lower" caste would not be willing to change places with a "higher" caste. Of course, each caste (skilled occupation) was accompanied by a set of social and economic advantages and disadvantages. For example, the moral responsibility of a noble or "higher" caste was to give material goods, upon request even if less wealthy, to a "lower" caste or else lose respect in the eyes of the populace. Obviously, this element of economic fairness reduced the level and possibilities of social conflict between traditional Black Afrikan occupations.

Without commenting upon the significance of race (i.e., the melanic factor) C.A. Diop describes the absolute differences between the acutely materialist and capitalist instincts of Europeans and the collectivisit instincts and egalitarian, representative politics of precolonial (pre-European) Black Afrikans. During the European Middle Ages, continuous socio-economic conflict occurred between the feudal landlords and peasants or merchant classes; likewise, in capitalist (post 1500 c.e.) Europe and EuropeanAmerica, prominent socio-economic clashes between the bourgeois (propertied) and proletariat (landless, manual workers) classes have been ongoing. It will come as no surprise to the reader that the hostile relations between grossly unequal socio-economic classes has been the driving force within European societies (see W. Rodney, How Europe Underdeveloped Africa, p. 39). For comparison purposes, the reader should recall the moral and economic responsibility of a "higher" caste to give material goods, upon request, to a "lower" caste (skilled occupation) in traditional, Black Afrikan societies.

The following documentation will show that, among the Europeans, feudal landlords and capitalist manufacturers, and landed ruling classes victimized the merchants, skilled laborers (artisans) and proletariat (i.e., peasants or landless, manual laborers), respectively. In closing, if the Afrikan (Black) reader of this text should absent-mindedly consider the possibility of a democratic reform of capitalist European-America, he/she might consider the words of Malcolm X (al hajj Malik Shabazz):

> ... A chicken cannot produce a duck egg, and a chicken can't produce a duck egg because the system itself was produced by a chicken egg and can only reproduce what produced it. The American system was produced from the enslavement of the Black man. This political, economic and social system of America was produced from the enslavement of the Black man and that particular system is capable only of reproducing that out of which itself was produced. (By Any Means Necessary, ed. by G. Breitman, p. 116).

> During the Middle Ages there evolved in
> European history a situation that has no parallel in
> Africa: the barbarian [Asiatic] invasions. It was

thus, under the threat of external danger against which protection at any cost was necessary, that European feudalism was born and grew concomitant with the seizure and occupation of land by the lords. During the Middle Ages, the entire feudal system was to be based on the possession of the land through the progressive despoiling of the protected inhabitants--creating the landed nobility--.... [The technique of the feudal system of exploitation was exceptionally inhumane in character, according to C.A. Diop]

Karl Marx showed in <u>Des Kapital</u> that the ... upheaval which was to give birth to modern capitalism began at the end of the 15th century, especially in England. Royalty and the parliament went to war against the feudal lords to try to win back central authority. Against the violent repression of the king and parliament, feudal lords reacted by progressively confiscating the lands of all the peasants who were tilling the soil under 'feudal tenure': serfdom was no more. Those formerly bound to the soil were now independent peasants. Overnight, there was thus created a proletariat without either hearth or home. Then these peasants were driven into the cities. The movement of expropriation spread to ecclesiastical communal domains by a system of 'enclosure.'

Conditions suitable for the birth of capitalism had been created. In becoming a wage-earner, the peasant no longer had anything but the strength of his labour to sell to the urban manufacturers or country farmers; he could no longer produce at home the things he needed for domestic use, but had to buy them as manufactured products on the home market which the capitalist circuit had established between the countryside and city. Of course, the newly created proletariat was not entirely and automatically absorbed by industry.

The unemployment which resulted turned a great many individuals into vagabonds, thieves, or vagrants, as they were called. This ever increasing flood of unemployed hands finally frightened the masters of industry. So a panic took hold of parliamentary legislators and led them to pass laws so terrible ... 72,000 vagrants were thus executed during that reign [of King Henry 8th of England, ca. 1530 c.e.]. An idler caught on the highway was branded on the chest with a V (for vagrant) and returned to his native city, whose slave he became, doing municipal work without pay, held in irons.[24]

As sheep raising became more profitable [during the closing years of the 15th century], much land was converted from tillage to pasturage, and large numbers of peasants were displaced by an emerging entrepreneurial gentry which either bought their land or cheated them out of it. Mass disturbances [in the West] erupted during the long transition from feudalism to capitalism beginning in the 16th century. To deal with these threats to civil order, many localities legislated severe penalties against vagrancy. Even before the 16th century, magistrates of Basel [N.W. Switzerland] had defined 25 different categories of beggars, together with the appropriate punishments for each. Penalties for beggary were made more severe, ..., including an elaborate schedule for branding, enslavement, and execution for repeated offenders. Even so, by 1572 beggary was said to have reached alarming proportions...[25]

The harsh feudal [and capitalist] laws of England recognized 300 capital crimes. Typical hanging offenses included: picking a pocket for more than a shilling [i.e., approx. 1 dollar in 1982 U.S. currency]; shoplifting to the value of 5 shillings [5 dollars]; stealing a horse or a sheep; poaching rabbits on a gentlemen's estate. A piteous petition in 1667 prayed for transportation [to England's colonies] instead of the death sentence for a wife convicted of stealing goods valued at 3 shillings and 4 pence (Calendar of State Papers, Colonial Series, V, 1667 (?) c.e.).[26] Slaves of towns or parishes subsisted into the 19th century, under the name of roundsmen, as Marx points out. The same laws remained in force under the reign of [Queen] Elizabeth [1572 c.e.]. The situation was exactly the same under [King] James I: idlers were branded with the letter R (for Rogue) on their left shoulders. Only in 1715 a.d. was this legislation abolished in England. Similar laws existed in France.[27]

'We may today recognize the opening of the 16th century as a period of special economic stress, whether we emphasize the agrarian revolution that was dislocating the manorial [feudal] organization, or the growth of manufactures in towns, involving the production of an urban proletariat
[landless, manual workers or peasants], . . .'

Sir Thomas More [1478-1535 c.e.] described their [the dispossessed farmers'] plight in 1516: 'The husbandmen [and wives, children, young babes, etc.] be thrust out of their own, or else either by covin or fraud, or violent oppression they be put beside it, or by wrongs and injuries they be so wearied, that they be compelled to sell all.'

Population changes and agricultural and other natural disasters characterized life throughout the Middle Ages; the resulting economic distress was exacerbated by the vagaries of an evolving market [i.e., capitalist] economy. Consequently, turbulence among the poor reached a new pitch.

'When the sense of oppression became overwhelming, the popular feeling manifested itself in widespread organized tumults, disturbances, and insurrections, from Wat Tyler's rebellion of 1381, and Jack Cade's march on London of 1460, to the Pilgrimage of Grace of 1536, and the Kett Norfolk rising of 1549--all of them successfully put down, but sometimes, not without great struggle.' In 1529 food riots erupted, with 1,000s of the Lyonnais [French] looting granaries and the homes of the wealthy; in 1530, artisans and journeymen armed themselves and marched through the streets; in 1531, mobs of starving peasants literally overran the town. One account of the times describes famished peasants so gorging themselves as to die on the very doorsteps where they were fed.

Laborers' vulnerability was assured by laws prohibiting the workers from combining for the purpose of exerting influence to reduce hours or raise wages. In 1548, any organized efforts by laborers to fix wages and hours were prohibited. There were 40 such laws on the books by 1800. New statutes in 1799 and 1800 effectively prohibited all joint action by workers. A companion statute enacted by [British] Parliament in 1350 forbade laborers from traveling from their regular places of residence so long as any employer there wanted to hire them at whatever wage levels had previously been paid. Efforts to regulate the supply of labor by law persisted: in 1563, the principles of earlier statutes were reaffirmed in a law requiring the unemployed to work for any who wanted them, and empowering justices of the peace to fix maximum wages and to penalize any employer who paid in excess of the standard.[28] Adam Smith [17231790] added: 'We have no acts of Parliament against combining to lower the price of work; but many against combining to raise it'. [29]

In 1601, the Law of Settlement empowered local authorities to remove from their respective jurisdictions those newcomers whose assets were so few that they occupied a property renting for less than 10 pounds a year. 'Laws of Settlement ... regulated it [the flow of labor] in the interest of the employing class....' Through such coercive measures as these the government enforced work during the transition from feudal labor relations to [so-called] free-market labor relations, and enforced it on terms dictated by the employers. Laborers could not organize, they could not refuse work,.... Writing in 1776 in <u>An Inquiry Into the Nature and Causes of the</u> <u>Wealth of Nations,</u> Adam Smith testified as to the extent and effectiveness of these [labor] constraints: 'There is scarce a poor man in England of 40 years of age, I will venture to say, who has not in some part of his life felt himself cruelly oppressed by this ill contrived law of settlement.'

Massive agricultural dislocations occurred during the late 18th century. Most of the English agricultural population had by then lost its landholdings. During the late 18th and early 19th centuries the English countryside was periodically besieged by the turbulent masses of displaced poor and the towns were racked by Ludism, radicalism, trade-unionism, and Chartism. [By the late 18th century in England,] The vast majority of people were a landless proletariat, hiring out by the year to tenant farmers. This [the late 18th and early 19th centuries] was an era of brutal repression; indeed, in no other domestic matters was Parliament so active as in the elaboration of the criminal codes. At the same time, troops were spread across the country and quartered in barracks.

As for the distress of displaced laborers, laissez-faire [i.e., capitalist] commentators of the time pontificated that this was the necessary concomitant of economic productivity and progress.[30] In a European society in which subordination was considered essential, ... Edmund Burke could speak of the working classes as "miserable sheep" and Voltaire [could speak of the working class as] "canaille,".... With D. Ricardo [17721823] and T.R. Malthus [1776-1834], the notion of massive privation and great inequality became a basic [capitalist] premise. His [the ordinary individual's] normal expectation was to live on the edge of starvation. Progress would enhance the wealth of those who, generally speaking, were already rich but not that of the masses. These conclusions have claim to be considered the propositions on which modern [Western] economic thought was founded.[31]

To take advantage of rising prices and new [agricultural] techniques, big landowners moved to expand their holdings still further by buying up small farms and, armed with parliamentary 'Bills of Enclosure,' by usurping the common and waste lands which had enabled many small cottagers to survive. The margin of their [small cottagers'] subsistence ... [had been] provided by the common and waste lands, no which they gathered kindling, grazed animals, and hunted game to supplement their meager wages. For great numbers of agricultural workers, enclosure meant no land on which to grow subsistence crops to feed their families, no grazing land to produce wool ..., no fuel to heat their cottages, and new restrictions against hunting.[32] Without the phenomenon of expropriation [i.e., land theft or enclosure; Bills of Enclosure, etc.], capitalism would not have come to be.[33]

The landed gentry ruled Britain until 1832, and the manufacturing classes joined them as rulers afterwards.[34] Those who owned the new factories, or raw materials, ... or banks that served them, lived in mansions by which the 19th century is still remembered. Their workers lived in dark and noisome hovels, crowded on dirty and unpaved streets.... If the poor were becoming less poor [by the mid-19th century], this change was slight as compared with the growing contrast between the rich and POOR.[35] E. J. Hobsbawm [in Industry and Empire, Vol II, 1968] estimates that up to the 1850's, upwards of 10% of the English population were paupers. John Stuart Mill [1806-1873 c.e.] suggested in 1863: 'The poor man, in France, notwithstanding the charitable relief that he may get, has always before his eyes the possibility of death by starvation ...'[36]

Modern capitalism, whenever it may be found, is a European export and not the result of the natural local evolution. Hoarding, usury, and all forms of excessive concentration of individual wealth are only the reflection of social anxiety, the uncertainty about tomorrow, a sort of shield for oneself and one's kin against a cruel fate. It is in an individualistic society that we see the great growth of such a phenomenon: from the Aegean [ancient] period to our own day, that of the Europeans was the hardest, roughest, least clement. Without any margin of safety, one whose means give out sinks before the indifferent eyes of other. No politico-social education has so far radically changed the Occidental [i.e., Western] mind in this respect. The technical and intellectual progress due to constant and necessary business, the energy with which one must imperturbably amass ever more wealth, the development of mercantilism--all these seem to flow, in large part, from one same initial principle [i.e., individualism].[37]

It is estimated [1970 c.e.] that 1.6% of the [U.S.A.] population owns at least 32% of all assets, and nearly all the investment assets; and 50% of the population owns practically nothing. It cannot be said that power in the U.S.A. is in the hands of the most qualified, since most of the wealth is inherited, and its possession, therefore, does not necessarily denote merit.[38] Individuals with taxable income of more than $1 million--35,875 in all--made up less than 0.04 of America's 103.3 million taxpayers [that is, 1 out of every 2,880 taxpayers] in 1986, but they claimed net capital gains of $135 billion, or one-third of all capital gains [i.e., profits on sales of stocks, bonds and certain other investments] claimed in 1986, the most recent IRS [U.S. Internal Revenue Service] data show.[39] Figures are piling up showing that the rich are getting much richer and the poor much poorer.... According to a report by the Center on Budget and Policy Priorities, ..., the gap between the wealthiest and poorest [U.S.] families has now reached its widest point since the bureau began accumulating this data in 1947. The income share of those families [i.e., the wealthiest 1/5th of the U.S.
population] increased to 43.7 percent of all national income in 1987 from 41.1 percent in 1973, while the income share of the lowest fifth declined to 4.6 percent from 5.5 percent.[40]

170

Chapter 8

A Poem for Black Minds

"A Poem for Black Hearts," by LeRoi Jones (Taken from <u>I Am the Darker</u> <u>Brother: An Anthology of Modern Poems by Black Americans</u>, ed. Arnold Adoff, Collier Books, New York City, 1968):

> For Malcolm's eyes, when they
> broke the face of some dumb white
> man. For Malcolm's hands raised
> to bless us all black and strong in
> his image of ourselves, for
> Malcolm's words fire darts, the
> victor's tireless thrust, words hung
> above the world change as it may,
> he said it, and for this he was
> killed, for saying and feeling, and
> being change, all collected hot in
> his heart, For Malcolm's heart,
> raising us above our filthy cities,
> for his stride, and his beat, and his
> address to the grey monsters of the
> world, For Malcolm's pleas for
> your dignity, black men, for your
> life, black men, for the filling of
> your minds with righteousness, For
> all of him dead and gone and
> vanished from us, and all of him
> which clings to our speech black
> god of our time. For all of him, and
> all of yourself, look up, black man,
> quit stuttering and shuffling, look
> up, black man, quit whining and
> stooping, for all of him, for Great
> Malcolm a prince of the earth, let

nothing in us rest until we avenge
ourselves for his death, stupid
animals that killed him, let us
never breathe a pure breath if we
fail, and white men call us faggots
til the end of the earth.

End Notes

Chapter One

1. Diop, "The Beginnings of Man and Civilization: Lecture by Diop in the M.L. King Jr. Intl. Chapel," trans Edward F. Taylor, in Van Sertima and Williams, p. 328.
2. Diop, "Listervelt Middleton Interviews Diop," trans. Elizabeth Clement, in Van Sertima and Williams, p. 287.
3. R.E. Leakey and R. Lewin, Origins (New York: E.P. Dutton, 1977), pp. 48-49. Scientific research notwithstanding, biochemist V. Sarich says "people just do not want to acknowledge their close kinship with apes, either anatomical or behavioral." Is this "species chauvinism?"
4. Diop, "The Beginnings of Man," in Van Sertima and Williams, pp. 323-32. See also "Puzzling Out Man's Ascent," Time, 7 Nov. 1977, pp. 64-78.
5. Diop, "L. Middleton Interviews Diop," in VanSertima and Williams, p286.
6. Diop, "The Beginnings of Man," pp. 323-325. Harvard paleoanthropologist David Pilbeam agrees with both dates-- 120,000 and 40,000 b.c.e.--for the existence of Homo sapiens and Homo sapiens-sapiens, respectively.
7. Leakey and Lewin, Origins, pp. 111-127, 128-129.
8. Akbar et al., pp. 8-9. Cf. V.N. Jones, "The Fragile X" [Chromosome]: Mother/Son Link to Retardation," Rocky Mountain. News, 25 Jan. 1984, pp. 51,53.
9. Diop, "Origin of the Ancient Egyptians," in Van Sertima and Williams, p. 35.
10. J.C. deGraft-Johnson, African Glory (Baltimore: Black Classic Press, 1954), pp. 3-.

11. .J.A. Rogers, Your History from the Beginning of Time to the Present (1940; rpt. Baltimore: Black Classic Press, 1983), p. 25.
12. Diop, Cultural Unity, pp. 128-131.
13. Diop, "L. Middleton Interviews Diop," p. 285.
14. Leakey and Lewin, 129.
15. Diop, "The Beginnings of Man," pp. 323-325, 328.
16. Diop, "Origin of the Ancient Egyptians," p. 54.
17. Shawna Moore, "Interview with Cheikh Anta Diop," in Van Sertima and Williams, pp. 240,242. The first appearance of the White race has since been calculated at 30,000 b.c.e. (before the Christian era), according to I. Van Sertima and L. Williams. 18   Diop, Cultural Unity, p. 66.
19. Diop, Black Africa, pp. 3-4.
20 Cheikh A. Diop, Precolonial Black Africa, trans. H.J. Salemson (Westport: Lawrence Hill and Co., 1987), pp. 212-215,229-233.
21. Diop, Cultural Unity, p. 183.

Chapter Two

1. Madhubuti, pp. 49-50.
2. Cheikh Diop, "The Introduction and First Two Chapters from His Last Book, Civilization or Barbarism: An Authentic Anthropology," trans. Edward F. Taylor, in Van Sertima and Williams, pp. 162-164.
3. Madhubuti, pp. 48-49.
4. Diop, "Introduction and First Two Chapters," p. 162.
5. Dr. Cheikh Anta Diop, "Nile Valley Committee Interviews Diop," in Van Sertima and Williams, pp. 292-293.
6. C. Diop, "Africa's Contribution to the Exact Sciences," trans. Irene D'Almeida, in Van Sertima and Williams, p. 86.
7. Diop, Cultural Unity, p. 58. Elsewhere, Diop adds that the Egyptians had created already a completely accurate solar calendar by 4245 or 4236 (with a slight adjustment) b.c.e. Thousands of years had been required to construct this Egyptian calendar.
8. Homer W. Smith, Man and His Gods (Boston: Little, Brown, and Co., 1953), pp. 11,24. See also J.G. Jackson, Introduction to African Civilizations, pp. 121-122.
9. George G.M. James, Stolen Legacy (San Francisco: J. Richardson Assoc., 1976), pp. 33-35.
10. R.T. Rundle Clark, Myth and Symbol in Ancient Egypt (London: Thames and Hudson Ltd., 1959), p. 31.
11. James, pp. 33-35.
12. J.T. Sporry, The Story of Egypt, n.p., n.d. Between 2780 and 2680 b.c.e. (before the

Christian era) under the reign of Pharaoh Djoser, philosopher-physician-architect Imhotep designed and engineered the building of the first "step" pyramid at Sakharta, which inaugurated the Great Pyramid Age--see Dr. ben-Jochannan, Africa: Mother of Western Civilization, pp. 271,315,317,475.

13. Diop, "Africa's Contribution," pp. 74,76,78,80.
14. J.A. Rogers, World's Great Men of Color, Vol. I (New York: McMillian Publishing Co., 1972), p. 39.
15. Chancellor Williams, p. 313.
16. Diop, The African Origin, pp. 234-235,250.
17. Madhubuti, p. 29.
18. Diop, "Origin of the Ancient Egyptians," in Van Sertima and Williams, pp. 41,44.
19. Rogers, World's Great Men, pp. 119,120.
20. F.M. Snowden, Blacks in Antiquity (Cambridge: Harvard Univ. Press, 1970), pp. 5,12-13.
21. deTocqueville, p. 355.
22. Leakey and Lewin, p. 114.
23. Diop, "The Beginnings of Man," in Van Sertima and Williams, p. 331.
24. Sporry, n.p. See also Diop, The African Origin, p. 22.
25. deGraft-Johnson, pp. 3-4.
26. Rogers, Your History, p. 4.
27. Leakey and Lewin, p. 136.
28. Diop, Cultural Unity, pp. 106,108,111.29.
29. Diop, The African Origin, p. 100.
30. J.G. Jackson, Introduction to African Civilizations (Secaucus: The Citadel Press, 1970), p. 62. Lewis Henry Morgan is quoted.

31. Diop, "Iron in the Ancient Egyptian Empire," trans. Darryl Provost, in Van Sertima and Williams, pp. 64-72.
32. Diop, Precolonial Black Africa, pp. 204-205.
33. C. Moore, "Interviews with Diop," in Van Sertima and Williams, pp. 263-265.
34. Diop, "The Introduction and First Two Chapters," pp. 162-164.
35. Smith, p. 50.
36. J.H. Carruthers, Essays in Ancient Egyptian Studies (Los Angeles: Timbuktu Publishing, 1984), pp. 94,105-106.
37. Smith, pp. 48-49. See also Dr. Carruthers, p. 92.
38. Sporry, n.p. See also Diop, African Origin, pp. 289-290; Carruthers, Essays, pp. 90103; Dr. A.G. Hilliard at al., eds., Teachings of Ptahhotep, pp. 16-37. Cf. J.A.

    Wilson, trans., "The Instructions of King Amen-em-het," in Ancient Near Eastern Texts Relating to the Old Testament, by ed. J.B. Pritchard, pp. 418-419.
39. Diop, Cultural Unity, pp. 150, 154-155.
40. Earl W. Faruq, "The Power of the Spiritual Dimension in Ancient Egyptian City Life," in Karenga and Carruthers, p. 73.
41. Diop, Cultural Unity, p. 163.
42. Snowden, Blacks in Antiquity, pp. 144-148,289-290.
43. F.M Snowden, Before Color Prejudice (Cambridge: Harvard Univ. Press, 1983), pp. 41-42.
44. Dr. Snowden, Blacks in Antiquity, pp. 144-145.
45. Diop, Cultural Unity, p. 57.
46. Diop, Cultural Unity, pp. iv,34,47,86.
47. Rogers, World's Great Men, pp. 36,37.

48. Diop, Cultural Unity, pp. 60,120,139.
49. Diop, African Origin, pp. 53-54.
50. Diop, Cultural Unity, p. 201.
51. Faruq, p. 73.
52. Diop, Cultural Unity, pp. 163-164.
53. Diop, "The Beginnings of Man," p. 342.
54. Diop, Cultural Unity, p. 65.
55. Diop, "The Beginnings of Man," pp. 342-343.
56. Diop, Cultural Unity, p. 202.
57. R. Graves and R. Patai, Hebrew Myths (Garden City: Doubleday and Co., 1963), p. 262.
58. E.A.W. Budge, The Mummy (New York City: Collier Books, 1972), p. 45.
59. Sporry, n.p. See also Dr. ben-Jochannan, Black Man of the Nile, pp. 238-239; Budge, The Mummy, 46.47.
60. Diop, "The Beginnings of Man," p. 341.
61. Diop, African Origin, pp. 248-249.
62. Snowden, Blacks in Antiquity, p. 104.

Chapter Three

1. deTocqueville, p. 355.
2. Diop, <u>Cultural Unity</u>, pp. 29, 200.
3. Rogers, <u>World's Great Men</u>, p. 2.
4. Diop, <u>Cultural Unity</u>, pp. 163-164, 194, 93.
5. Madhubuti, p. 30.
6. Diop, <u>Cultural Unity</u>, pp. 144-146, 157-158.
7. Afterword by Spady, in <u>Cultural Unity</u>, by Diop, p. 230.
8. Diop, <u>Precolonial Black Africa</u>, p. 21.
9. Diop, <u>African Origin</u>, p. 142.
10. Diop, <u>Precolonial Black Africa</u>, pp. 21-24.
11. Graves and Patai, p. 17.
12. Diop, <u>Precolonial Black Africa</u>, pp. 18-19.
13. Diop, <u>Cultural Unity</u>, p. 134.
14. Diop, <u>Cultural Unity</u>, p. 45, 144.
15. Graves and Patai, p. 15.
16. Diop, <u>Cultural Unity</u>, pp. 132-134, 139-140.
17. Diop, <u>Cultural Unity</u>, pp. 77, 154, 155, 200.
18. Diop, "Africa's Contribution," in Van Sertima and Williams, pp. 79, 87.
19. Diop, <u>Cultural Unity</u>, p. 206.
20. Diop, "Africa's Contribution," p. 79.
21. James, pp. 56-57, 71.
22. Diop, <u>Cultural Unity</u>, pp. 160 161.
23. James, p. 87.
24. Diop, "Africa's Contribution," pp. 86, 87.
25. Rogers, <u>World's Great Men</u>, p. 40.

26. Diop, "Africa's Contribution," pp. 75, 83-84.
27. Diop, Cultural Unity, p. 207.
28. Diop, "Africa's Contribution," pp. 75, 82.
29. Diop, "The Beginnings of Man," in Van Sertima and Williams, p. 346.
30. Diop, "Africa's Contribution," pp. 75-76.
31. Diop, Cultural Unity, pp. 205-206.
32. Diop, Precolonial Black Africa, pp. 31-32.
33. Diop, Cultural Unity, p. 158.
34. James, p. 145. See also Jackson, African Civilizations, pp. 98-102.
35. Diop, "Africa's Contribution," p. 82.
36. James, pp. 56-57, 64, 68, 70-72, 148, 168, 172.
37. James, pp. 28, 135.
38. Diop, Precolonial Black Africa, pp. 35-37, 40-41, 178.
39. See also Jackson, pp. 117-121; Diop, Cultural Unity, pp. 207-208.

Chapter Four

1. Sigmund Freud, The Future of an Illusion, trans. J. Strachey (NYC: W.W. Norton, 1961), p. 30. See also J.M. Robertson, Pagan Christs, p. 15.
2. Y. ben-Jochannan, Our Black Seminarians and Black Clergy without a Black Theology (NYC: Alkebu-lan Books, 1978), p.iv. Cf. Robertson, p. 13.
3. James, pp. 50-51.
4. J.G. Frazer, The New Golden Bough, ed. T.H. Gaster (NYC: Mentor, 1964), p. 422.
5. Freud, p. 22.
6. Frazer, pp. 35-187, 273-274. See also Robertson, Pagan Christs, pp. 14-15.
7. Freud, pp. 15-20, 21-24.
8. Diop, Cultural Unity, p. 159.
9. Clark, pp. 25, 30, 31, 58, 79. Likewise, Diop says all the technological and cultural elements of ancient Egyptian (Kemit; Ta-Merrian) civilization were already in place by the Third Dynasty (ca. 2780 b.c.e.) of the Old Kingdom.
10. Nobles, "Ancient Egyptian Thought," in Karenga and Carruthers, p. 105. See also Dr. Maulana Karenga, "[God] Ra's Description of His Creation," in Selections from the Husia, pp. 3, 5-7.
11. Y. ben-Jochannan et al., Understanding the African Philosophical Concept behind the "Diagram of the Law of Opposites" (NYC: Alkebu-lan Books, 1975), p. 23.
12. Clark, pp. 37-38, 74. See also J.A. Wilson, trans., "Another Version of Creation by [God] Atum," in Ancient ... Texts Relating to the Old Testament, by Pritchard, pp. 34.

13. ben-Jochannan, <u>Our Black Seminarians</u>, pp. 28-29.
14. Diop, "The Beginnings of Man," in Van Sertima and Williams, p. 339.
15. Diop, <u>Cultural Unity</u>, p. 159.
16. Smith, pp. 59-60. See also S. Freud, <u>Moses and Monotheism</u>, pp. 21-26.
17. Graves and Patai, p. 27.
18. Smith, p. 113.
19. James, p. 67. See also Jackson, <u>African Civilizations</u>, p. 111.
20. Smith, p. 96. Psychiatrist/religious scholar Sigmund Freud says <u>no</u> historian can regard the Biblical account of Moses as other than a pious myth.
21. Clark, pp. 31-32, 166.
22. Diop, "The Beginnings of Man," in Van Sertima and Williams, p. 344. See also Freud, <u>Moses and Monotheism</u>, pp. 27, 28-29.
23. Diop, <u>Precolonial Black Africa</u>, pp. 225-226.
24. Diop, <u>Cultural Unity</u>, p. 42.
25. Frazer, p. 341. See also Jackson, pp. 129-130.
26. Clark, pp. 112-113, 235.
27. Frazer, pp. 389, 403-404. See also Robertson, <u>Pagan Christs</u>, p. 52. Egyptologist E.A.W. Budge says Egyptians proclaimed the resurrection of a spiritual body and the immortality of the soul, more than 5,000 years ago.
28. Diop, <u>Precolonial Black Africa</u>, pp. 30-34.
29. ben-Jochannan, <u>Our Black Seminarians</u>, pp. xii, xlvi, liv.
30. Diop, "Africa's Contribution," in Van Sertima and Williams, p. 83. See also Jackson, pp. 132-133, 144-146; Robertson, p. 68.

31. ben-Jochannan, Black Man, pp. 125-126. See also Robertson, p. 52-53, 68.

32. Smith, pp. 52, 99-100. Although he deduces that ancient Jews received the monotheistic principle from the Egyptians, Freud states--citing other historians--that Yahweh was a volcano-god borrowed by the Jews from a Middle-East, Arabic tribe.

33. Graves and Patai, pp. 24-25, 27-28. In short, the two Genesis version of creation differ in the order of Hebrew-God Yahweh's creations and the length thereof, respectively.

34. Smith, pp. 91, 116-117.

35. Graves and Patai, pp. 15, 145. See also John A. Wilson, trans., "The [Egyptian] Story of Two Brothers," in The Ancient Near East, by ed. J.B. Pritchard, pp. 12-16.

36. ben-Jochannan, African Origins of the Major "Western Religions" (NYC: Alkebulan Books, 1973), pp. 15, 61, 63. See also Freud, Moses, pp. 29-31.

37. See also Pritchard, Archaeology and the Old Testament, pp. 165, 170; Afterword J.H. Marks, in Gilgamesh, by H. Mason, pp. 117-125.

38. ben-Jochannan, African Origins, pp. 119-201, 212, 214-215.

Chapter Five

1. Clark, p. 26.
2. Snowden, <u>Blacks in Antiquity</u>, pp. 136-141. The emphasis, or underlining, is mine.
3. deGraft Johnson, p. 59.
4. Snowden, <u>Blacks in Antiquity</u>, pp. 136-141.
5. ben-Jochannan, <u>African Origins</u>, p. 72.
6. Graves and Patai, pp. 15, 122, 145.
7. deGraft Johnson, pp. 11-12. See also Jackson, pp. 107-108; John A. Wilson, trans., "The [Caucasian] Hyksos in Egypt," in <u>Ancient Texts Relating to the Old Testament</u>, by Pritchard, pp. 230-234.
8. Smith, p. 89. Compare A. Joseph Ben-Levi, "The First and Second Intermediate Periods in Kemetic History," Karenga and Carruthers, pp. 55-68, concerning the origin, ethnicity, and dating of the Caucasoid Habiru and Hyksos invaders.
9. Graves and Patai, pp. 13-14.
10. Smith, p. 89. Compare: Budge, p. 23-29; J.A. Wilson, trans., "The [Egyptian] War Against the [Caucasian] Peoples of the Sea," in <u>The Ancient Near East</u>, p. James B. Pritchard, pp. 185-186.
11. deGraft Johnson, pp. 11-12.
12. Smith, pp. 95-96. Freud says <u>no</u> historian can regard the Biblical account of the Exodus as more than a religious myth (<u>Moses and Monotheism</u>, p. 38).
13. ben-Jochannan, <u>Black Man</u>, pp. 237-238, 357-358.
14. Jackson, pp. 167-170.
15. deGraft Johnson, pp. 65, 66-67. Historian Jane Soames is quoted.

16. Introd. by Dr. J. Henrik Clarke, in Cultural Unity, by Diop, p. x.
17. Dr. ben-Jochannan goes further: In Africa: Mother of W. Civilization, pp. 150-152, 401-402, he states that Afrikan Moors (Blacks) translated texts on science, medicine, pharmacology, astronomy, mathematics, ethics, philosophy, metaphysics, music, etc. from the ancient Egyptian hieroglyphics into Arabic. Copernicus, Roger Bacon, and Johann Kepler, to name a few, were some of the most famous medieval-European scientists who received the knowledge of their basic science from the works of Afrikan Moors.
18. deGraft Johnson, pp. 82-84, 86-87.
19. Diop, Cultural Unity, p. 69.
20. Diop, Precolonial Black Africa, pp. 48, 50, 55, 63, 66-69, 101, 163-164.
21. Diop, Cultural Unity, pp. 68-69, 125.
22. ben-Jochannan, African Origins, pp. 59-60.
23. To repeat, R. Graves and R. Patai state the following about the Hebrew (Judaic Old Testament), Negrophobic Ham-myth: "That Negroes are doomed to serve men of lighter colour [i.e., Caucasians] was a view gratefully borrowed by Christians in the Middle [Medieval] Ages: a severed shortage of cheap labour, caused by plague, made the [European] re-institution of slavery attractive (Hebrew Myths, p. 122)."
24. deGraft Johnson, p. 127.
25. Eric Williams, p. 202.
26. deGraft Johnson, pp. 49-51. The European J.M. Robertson, in Pagan Christs, pp. 1517, adds that the progress of a religious system is largely influenced by political (e.g., military, economic) factors, as opposed to spiritual or intellectual factors.

Chapter Six

1. Diop, <u>Precolonial Black Africa</u>, p. 130.
2. Rodney, pp. 41-43.
3. Diop, <u>Precolonial Black Africa</u>, pp. 134-135, 140, 184.
4. Diop, <u>Cultural Unity</u>, pp. 164-165.
5. deGraft-Johnson, pp. 152-153.
6. Chancellor Williams, pp. 235, 270-271, 318.
7. Madhubuti, pp. 27, 112.
8. Eric Williams, pp. 26, 108.
9. Malcolm X, p. 123.
10. Madhubuti, p. 27. Dr. Haki is quoting Joann Duggan et. al.
11. Eric Williams, pp. 1x, 52, 98-99, 101-102, 105, 209.
12. Chancellor Williams, p. 274.
13. Eric Williams, p. 202.
14. deGraft-Johnson, p. 160.
15. Malcolm X, pp. 80, 124.
16. F.F. Piven and R.A. Cloward, <u>Regulating the Poor</u> (New York: Vintage Books, 1971), p. 236-237.
17. Rogers, <u>Your History</u>, p. 75.
18. Madhubuti, pp. 27, 32, 204-205.
19. Chancellor Williams, p. 272.
20. Diop, <u>Precolonial B. Africa</u>, p. 142.21.
21. Malcolm X, p. 28.
22. Madhubuti, pp. 13-14.
23. Wright, p. 30.
24. Madhubuti, pp. 18, 37-38.

25. deGraft-Johnson, pp. 110-119. Has history repeated itself? Has Libyan (i.e., Arab or Caucasoid) ruler Colonial Moammar Khadafy's 1980's military intervention into the Black Afrikan nation Chad been repeat of the greedy land-theft instinct of Mulay Ahmed El Mansur, the Sultan of Morocco, whose prolonged 16th and 17th century invasion of Songhai signaled the destabilization and destruction of that West Afrikan Empire? If history does repeat itself, then Blacks worldwide might do well also to observe the millennium-old battle of the Muslim Arabs--of northern Sudan--against the Black traditionalists--of southern Sudan--which continues to this day. See also A. Cowell, "Unrest in the Sudan: An Isolated Egypt?" The [Louisville] Courier Journal, 20 Oct. 1981, Sec. A, p. 15; Chancellor Williams, pp. 312-313.

26. Carlos Moore, "Interviews with Diop," in Van Sertima and Williams, p. 275.

27. Rogers, World's Great Men, pp. 394-397.

28. Nkrumah, p. 59.

29. Rodney, pp. 228, 229.

30. Nkrumah, p. 59.

31. Rodney, pp. 236-238.

32. Carlos Moore, "Interviews with Diop," pp. 271, 273-274.

33. Madhubuti, pp. 105-106, 212.34.

34. Rodney, p. 235.

35. Postscript by A.M. Babu, in Europe Underdeveloped Africa, by Rodney, p. 287. See also N. Chomsky and E. Herman, The Washington [D.C.] Connection and Third World Fascism, p. 50.

36. Diop, Black Africa, pp. 15, 22, 31. See also B. Moyers, The Secret Government-The [U.S.] Constitution in Crisis, pp. 9-10.

37. Babu, in <u>Europe Underdeveloped Africa</u>, by Rodney, pp. 283-285.

Chapter Seven

1. Diop, Precolonial Black Africa, p. 158.
2. Rodney, p. 255.
3. Diop, Precolonial Black Africa, p. 160.
4. Smith, p. 8.
5. Diop, Cultural Unity, pp. 147, 149, 179-180, 195.
6. Afterword by Spady, in Cultural Unity, by Diop, p. 230.
7. J. Kenneth Galbraith, The Affluent Society (New York: Mentor Books, 1984), pp. 1, 2, 4, 24.
8. Diop, Precolonial Black Africa, pp. 10, 13-15, 24.
9. Rodney, p. 38.
10. Snowden, Before Color Prejudice, p. 70.
11. Rodney, pp. 37-38. Dr. Rodney says there were few slaves and no epoch of slavery in traditional Afrika.
12. Eric Williams, p. 5.
13. Madhubuti, pp. 100, 105.
14. Nkrumah, p. 13.
15. Diop, Precolonial Black Africa, pp. 6, 82, 105-106, 134-137, 141-142.
16. Rodney, pp. 39, 41.
17. Nkrumah, p. 13. Describing the pre-European personality of Black Afrikans, poethistorian Aime Cesaire wrote the following in 1948: "From the untroubled private citizen to almost fabulous leader there was an unbroken chain of understanding and trust. Their customs were pleasing, built on unity, kindness, respect for age. No coercion, only mutual assistance, the joy of living, a free acceptance of discipline."

18. Diop, Precolonial Black Africa, pp. 9-11, 59-60, 102-103, 148-150.
19. Diop, Precolonial Black Africa, pp. 99-100.
20. Nkrumah, p. 22.
21. Diop, Precolonial Black Africa, pp. 65, 108, 181-182.
22. Nkrumah, p. 14.
23. Diop, Precolonial Black Africa, pp. 72-75.
24. Diop, Precolonial Black Africa, pp. 101-103, 143-146.
25. Piven and Cloward, pp. 8, 12, 15.
26. Eric Williams, pp. 11-12.
27. Diop, Precolonial Black Africa, p. 146.
28. Piven and Cloward, pp. 10, 12-14, 19, 37.
29. Galbraith, p. 19.
30. Piven and Cloward, pp. 17, 20, 37.
31. Galbraith, pp. 17, 20, 27.
32. Piven and Cloward, pp. 17-18.
33. Diop, Precolonial Black Africa, p. 147.
34. Piven and Cloward, p. 38.
35. Galbraith, p. 18.
36. Piven and Cloward, pp. 21, 22.
37. Diop, Precolonial Black Africa, pp. 148, 158-159.
38. Nkrumah, pp. 33-34. In their 1971 text, F. Piven and R. Cloward indicate that, during the evolution of capitalism, the so-called free-enterprise market provided little or no reward for most workers and that this is still so for many.
39. "Bush Likely to Win Fight Over Capital Gains," The Denver Post, 29 July 1989, Sec. A, p. 1.
40. "CEO [Chief Executive Officer] Pay Breaks $1 Million Barrier," The Denver Post, 16 July 1989. See

also A.F. Brimmer, "Income and Wealth," <u>Ebony</u>, August 1987, pp. 42-48; J. Kozol, "The New Untouchables," <u>Newsweek: Special Issue</u>, Winter/Spring, 1990, pp. 48-49: "Meanwhile, the gulf in income between rich and poor families is wider than at any time since figures were recorded, starting in the 1940's. The richest 20% received 44% of national family income; the poorest 20% got only 4.6%.

Note: In closing, I would add one remark to prevent, perhaps, an unsure reader from failing to see the "forest for the trees:" Psychoanalytically speaking, whether the destructive traits of Caucasians occur from a genetically transmitted collectiveunconscious (a la European-psychologist Carl Jung) or whether they result from a collectively socialized unconscious, the result is the same--over the past 4,000 years of recorded history, Whites have sought incessantly to control and destroy Blacks (Afrikans) and their civilizations.

A Brief List of Articles and Pamphlets Consulted

"Anthropologist Disputes Identification of New Human Species." [Louisville] Courier-Journal, 11 Feb. 1979, Sec. A, p. 7.

Antiquity Unveiled: Ancient Voices from the Spirit Realms Disclose the Most Startling Revelations, Proving Christianity to be of Heathen Origin. 1892; reprint. Philadelphia: Oriental Publishing Co.

Balouny, Lisette. "Guerrilas in Chad Vow to make Libyans Leave." [Louisville] Courier-Journal, 29 March 1981, Sec. D, p. 4.

Billingsley, Andrew. The Evolution of the Black Family. New York: National Urban League, 1976.

Boyd, Gerald M. "Cities' Poor Missing Out of Recovery." Denver Post, 18 Dec. 1983, Sec. A, p. 23.

Brimmer, Andrew F. "Income and Wealth." Ebony, August 1987, pp. 42-48.

Bryce, Herringon J. Economic Progress of Blacks after 200 Years. New York: National Urban League, 1976.

"Bush Likely to Win Fight over Capital Gains." Denver Post, 29 July 1989, Sec. A, p. 1.

"Census Says Poverty Rise Steady Since 1979." Rocky Mountain News, 24 Feb. 1984, p. 4.

"CEO Pay Breaks $1 Million Barrier." Denver Post, 16 July 1989.

"Chad: Desert Standoff." Time, 5 Sep. 1983, p. 36.

Cowell, Alan. "N'Djamena: French Flavors Capitol." [Louisville] CourierJournal, 14 Aug. 1983, Sec. A., p. 2.

_____ "Unrest in the Sudan: An Isolated Egypt?" [Louisville] Courier-Journal, 29 Oct. 1981, Sec. A, p. 15.

Darkwah, Doris. "The Role of Africa in the Rise of Judaism." Black Books Bulletin.

Edelman, M.W. "Save the Children." Ebony, August 1986, pp. 53-60.

Gupte, Pranay B. "African Leaders Condemn U.S. for 'Collusion' with South Africa." [Louisville] Courier-Journal, 28 June 1981, Sec. A, p. 2.

Hare, Nathan Ph.D. "Is the Black Middle Class Blowing It? ... Yes!" Ebony: Special Issue, August 1987, pp. 85-86.

Harsch, E. "Death Penalty: Supreme Court Sanctions More Legalized Murder." The Militant, 27 May 1987, p. 7.

Hotema, Prof. Hilton. Mystery Man of the Bible. Mokelumne Hill, Ca.: Health Research.

"Interview: Richard Leakey." Omni, March 1983, pp. 95-104, 142-145.

Jager, Fred G. "Coors and the NAACP Bury the Hatchet." The City Edition, 26 Sep. to Oct. 1984, p. 13.

Jones, Verna N. "The Fragile X: Mother/Son Link to Retardation." Rocky Mountain News, 25 Jan. 1984, pp. 51, 53.

Kaukas, Dick. "Man and Ape." Scene, 6 June 1981, p. 3.

Kozol, J. "The New Untouchables." Newsweek, Winter/Spring, 1990, pp. 48-49.

Kunjufu, Johari M. An African Frame of Reference. Chicago: Inst. of Pos. Educ.

Lacayo, R. "Clearing a Path to the Chair: The Supreme Court Rejects a Key Legal Challenge to the Death Penalty." Time, 4 May 1987, p. 80.

Lippman, Thomas. "South American Empire Steadily Spreads in

U.S." [Lousiville] Courier-Journal, 18 April 1982, Sec. E, p. 4.

MacRobert, A.M. "Toward a More Unequal Society." Westword, 12 Sep. 1984, pp. 12, 14.

McKean, Kevin. "Reading the Molecular Clock: The Record of Evolution may be Written in Proteins and Genes." Discover, July 1983, pp. 28-31.

_____ "Vincent Sarich: Preaching the Molecular Gospel." Discover, July 1983, pp. 34-40.

_____ and Shannon Brownlee. "Facing Up to Man's Past." Discover, July 1983, pp. 22-26.

Mitchell, Charles. "Diplomats Ruling Out Quick Fix of Chad War." Rocky Mountain News, 27 Nov. 1983, p. 85.

Mitchell, Constance. "USA Family Earnings Rise 7.6%." USA Today, 31 Jan. 1984, Sec. A, p. 2.

"More Minorities Stand in Poverty Line." Denver Post, 1 Sep. 1988, Sec. A, p. 2. "Nation's Poverty Rolls are Partly Swollen by President Reagan's Cuts in Aid to Poor." [Louisville] Courier-Journal, 18 March 1984, Opinion Section.

Peters, Tom. "Capitalism Needs a Few Venturesome Souls." Rocky Mountain News, 5 Sep. 1989, Sec. B, p. 12.

Pienciak, Richard T. "Sexual, Racial Bias Still Pervades Business, Study Says." [Louisville] Courier-Journal, 21 Jan. 1979, Sec. A, p. 16.

"Poverty Rate to Stay high, Economists Say." Denver Post, 19 Oct. 1983, Sec. A, p. 10.

"Puzzling Out Man's Ascent: A Young Leakey Carries on the Search for Human Origins." Time, 7 Nov. 1977, pp. 64-78.

"Racial Bias in Capital Punishment Discounted." Denver Post, 23 April 1987, Sec. A, pp. 1, 4.

Reinhold, Robert. "Mammal's Fossil is First Every Found in Antarctic." [Louisville] Courier-Journal, 21 March, 1982, Sec. A, pp. 1, 18.

Rensberger, Boyce. "When Man First Stood Upright: New Ideas." [Louisville] Courier-Journal, 11 Feb. 1979, Sec. D.

Rich, Spencer. "Poverty Rose in 1970's for Blacks, Report Says." [Louisville] Courier-Journal, 23 Jan. 1980, Sec. A, p. 4.

Rogal, Kim, et al. "The Colonel [Kaddafi] Strikes South." Newsweek, 22 Aug. 1983, pp. 24-26.

Rosenblatt, Robert A. "Jobless Rate Down to 8% in January." Denver Post, 4 Feb. 1984, Sec. C, p. 1.

Rosenthal, Robert J. "Khadafy's Aims are Obscure, But He's a Potent Threat in Africa." [Louisville] Times, 16 Aug. 1983, Sec. A, p. 13.

Ross, Jay. "Egypt's Neighbor [Sudan] is Thrust Into Danger Zone." [Louisville] Courier-Journal, 18 Oct. 1981, Sec. A, pp. 1, 24.

Samuelson, Robert J. "The American Job Machine." Newsweek, 23 Feb. 1987, p. 57.

Schilling, Thomas. "Coors Calls Blacks 'Intellectual' Inferiors." Rocky Mountain News, 24 Feb. 1984, p. 64.

and Chris Broderick. "Outraged Blacks Say Coors Insulted Entire Race." Rocky Mountain News, 25 Feb. 1984, p. 10.

Schmeck, Harold M., Jr. "Discovery Moves Man's Use of Fire Back a Million Years." [Louisville] Courier-Journal, 14 Nov. 1981, Sec. A, p. 3. "Scientific Creationism vs. Evolution." [Louisville] Courier-Journal, 6 Oct. 1980, Sec. A, p. 6.

Sheppard, Lee. "Tax Myths and the Middle Class." [Louisville] Courier-Journal, 13 July 1986, Sec. D, p. 3.

"The Significance of Race in Sentencing." Parade, 22 Jan. 1984, p. 13.

Thurow, Lester C. "A Rising Tide of Poverty." Newsweek, 11 July 1983, p. 62.

Tierney, John, et al. "The Search for Adam and Eve." Newsweek, 11 Jan. 1988, pp. 46-52.

Verrastro, Dominic. "Bootstraps Won't Do the Job For Many of the Poor." Rocky Mountain News, 4 May 1987, p. 46.

Vrazo, Fawn. "U.S. Blacks' Status Called a Disaster," Denver Post, 1 Jan 1984, Sec. A, p.1.

Webster, Bayard. "Primate Living 30 Million Years Ago Was Ancestor of Man, Scientists Say." [Louisville] Courier-Journal, 10 Feb 1978, Sec. A, p.2.

"Well-Off Kids Have Higher IQ's" Rocky Mountain News, 17 Aug 1989, p. 4.

"Women's 1970 to 1980 Pay Gap Up" Denver Post, 16 Jan 1984, Sec. A, pp. 1, 14.

A Partial List of Works Consulted

Adebisi, Kwesi. Black and Fact. Columbus, Oh.: The Family and Npingo (2) Coop, 1977.

"Back to Africa." Crisis. November, 1979.

ben-Jochannan, Dr. Yosef. The Alkebu-lanians of Ta-Merry's "Mysteries System," and the Ritualization of the Late Bro. Kwesi Adebisi. New York: Alkebu-lan Books, 1981.

_____. Black Mental Illness and the Bicentennial. 2 Vols. New York: Alkebulan Books, 1976.

_____. Cultural Genocide in the Black and African Studies Curriculum. New York: Alkebu-lan Books, 1973.

_____. In Pursuit of Geo. G.M. James' Study of African Origins in "Western Civilization." New York: Alkebu-lan Books, 1980.

_____, and George E. Simmonds. The Black Man's North and East Africa. New York: Alkebu-lan Books, 1972.

Bennett, Lerone. Pioneers in Protest. Baltimore: Pelican Books, 1979.

Boggs, James. The American Revolution: Pages from a Negro Worker's Notebook. New York: Modern Reader Paperbacks, 1968.

Budge, E.A. Wallis. The Egyptian Book of the Dead: The Papyrus of Ani in The British Museum; the Egyptian Text with Interlinear Transliteration and Translation. 1895; rpt. New York: Dover Publ., 1967.

_____. Osiris and the Egyptian Resurrection. 2 Vols. New York: Dover, 1973.

Bulfinch, Thomas. Bulfinch's Mythology: The Age of Fable, The Age of Chivalry, Legends of Charlemagne. New York: T.Y. Crowell, n.d.

Castro, Fidel. "Cuba's Internationalist Volunteers in Angola." New International, Vol. 2 (Fall 1985), pp. 119-135.

Coleman, M., ed. Black Children Just Keep on Growing: Alternative Curriculum Models for Young Black Children. Washington: Black Child Development Inst., 1977.

Colson, Andrew, ed. African Socialism in Practice: The Tanzanian Experience. Nottingham: Spokesman Publ., 1982.

Delany, Martin R. The Condition, Elevation, Emigration, and Destiny of the Colored People of the United States. New York: Arno Press, 1968.

Diaz, John. "Bitter Groff Condemns 'Prehistoric' [Colorado] Lawmakers: Lawmaker Blames Racism for Bill's Defeat." Denver Post, 25 Feb. 1987, Sec. A, pp. 1, 12.

"Dr. Frances Welsing on Racism." [Phil] Donahue. CBS, 1988.

DuBois, W.E.B. Black Reconstruction in America, 1860-1880. New York: Athenium, 1979.

_____. Dusk of Dawn: An Essay Toward an Autobiography of a Race Concept. 1971; rpt. New York: Schocken Books.

_____. The Souls of Black Folk: Essays and Sketches. Greenwich: Fawcett Publications, 1961.

"Early Life in Arctic is Reported." The Louisville Times, 16 Sep. 1983, Sec. A, p. 4.

Edwards, I.E.S. The Pyramids of Egypt. Rev. ed. New York: Penguin Books, 1979.

Erman, Adolf. The Literature of the Ancient Egyptians: Poems, Narratives, and Manuals of Instruction, from the Third and Second Millennia B.C. Trans. A.M. Blackman. New York: Benjamin Blom, 1971.

Fanon, Franz. Black Skin, White Masks. Trans. by C.L. Markmann. New York: Grove Press, 1967.

Fingerman, Milton. Animal Diversity. New York: Holt, Rinehart and Winston, 1969, pp. 159-166.

Freire, Paulo. Pedagogy of the Oppressed. NYC: Herder and Herder, 1971.

Fuller, Hoyt W. Journey to Africa. Chicago: Third World Press, 1972.

Hare, N., and J. Hare. The Endangered Black Family: Coping with the Unisexualization and Coming Extinction of the Black Race. San Francisco: Black Think Tank, 1984.

Hayes, Carlton J.H. et al. History of Western Civilization to 1650, Vol. 1. 2nd ed. United States: Collier-McMillian, 1969.

History and Military Affairs. 3 vols. Colorado: U.S. Air Force Academy, 1969.

Hunter, Jane. Israeli Foreign Policy: South Africa and Central America. Boston: South End Press, 1987.

Jackson, Dr. J.G. Ethiopia and the Origin of Civilization: A Critical Review of the Evidence of Archaeology, Anthropology, History and Comparative Religion... 1939; rpt. Baltimore: Black Classic Press.

Johanson, Donald D., and M.A. Edey. <u>Lucy: The Beginnings of Humankind</u>. New York: Warner Books, 1982.

Leakey, Richard E., and R. Lewin. <u>People of the Lake: Mankind and Its Beginnings</u>. Avon Press, n.d.

Lesko, Leonard. <u>The Ancient Egyptian Book of Two Ways</u>. Berkeley: Univ. of California Press, 1972.

<u>The Lost Books of the Bible and the Forgotten Books of Eden: Being All the Gospels, Epistles, and Other Pieces Now extant Attributed in the First Four Centuries to Jesus Christ, His Apostles and Their Companions Not Included, by Its Compilers, In the Authorized New Testament; ..., etc</u>. New York: New American Library, 1974.

Madhubuti, Dr. H. <u>From Plan to Planet</u>. Chicago: Third World Press.

Malcolm X. <u>Autobiography of Malcolm X</u>. With assistance of Alex Haley. New York: Grove Press, 1965.

_____. <u>The End of White World Supremacy: Four Speeches of Malcolm X</u>. Ed. Benjamin Goodman. Merlin House, 1971.

_____. <u>Malcolm X on Afro-American History</u>. 2nd ed. New York: Pathfinder Press, 1970.

_____. <u>Malcolm X Talks to Young People</u>. 2nd ed. New York: Pathfinder Press, 1988.

<u>Mystical Rites and Rituals</u>. Phoebus Publ. Co and Octopus Books, 1970-71.

"Noam Chomsky." <u>Bill Moyers' World of Ideas</u>. New York: Journal Graphics, 1988.

Onwuachi, Chike. <u>Black Ideology in the African Diaspora</u>. Chicago: Third World Press, 1973.

Onwuejeogwu, M. Angulu. The Social Anthropology of Africa: An Introduction. London: Heinemann Books, 1975.

Padmore, George. Pan-Africanism or Communism? The Coming Struggle for Africa. New York: Roy Publ., 1956.

"Renaissance." In "Ideas and Beliefs." Information Please Almanac. 1987 ed., pp. 448-449.

Riggs, Marlon. Ethnic Notions: Portraits of Prejudice. PBS/KQED/WNET, 3 Feb., 1988.

Rogers, J.A. World's Great Men of Color, Vol 2. New York: Macmillan Co., 1972.

_____. 100 Amazing Facts about the Negro with Complete Proof: A Short Cut to the World History of the Negro. 1957; rpt. St. Petersburg, Fl.: Helga M. Rogers, 1985.

_____, The Five Negro Presidents, According to What White People Said They Were. New York: H.M. Rogers, 1965.

Shinnie, P.L. The African Iron Age. Oxford Univ. Press, 1971.

Simons, A. "Former Agent Comes in from the Cold: Home from Exile, Philip Agee Picks Up His Campaign Against the CIA." Up-the-Creek, 13 Nov. 1987, p. 10.

Steyaert, T. Life and Patterns of Order. McGraw-Hill Publ., 1971, pp. 439-440, 472-484.

Tambo, Oliver [Afrikan National Congress President]. "The Future Belongs to the Majority." New International, Vol 2 (Fall 1985), pp. 69-83.

Ullmann, Owen. "Jobless Rate Off to 8.2% at Year End." Denver Post, 7 Jan. 1984, Sec. A, pp. 1, 4.

Welsing, Frances Cress, M.D. <u>Ballgames as Symbols in the White Supremacy System and Culture</u>. Monograph, n.p., n.d.

_____ . <u>The Mother Fucker and the Original Mother Fucker</u>... n.p., n.d.

_____ . "Women Moving Toward the 21st Century." <u>Ebony</u>, 1975.

Wobogo, Vulinedela. "Diop's Two Cradle Theory and the Origin of White Racism." <u>Black Books Bulletin</u>, Vol. 4 (Winter 1976).

Note: The reader will understand I am unable to list all the relevant texts and articles consulted during the past 15 years.

Bibliography

A List of Works Cited

Agee, Philip. Inside the Company: CIA Diary. New York: Bantam, 1981.

Akbar, Na'im, et al. Voodoo or IQ: An Introduction to African Psychology. Chicago: Inst. of Positive Education, 1979.

ben-Jochannan, Dr. Yosef A.A. Africa: Mother of Western Civilization. Baltimore: Black Classic Press, 1988.

_____. African Origins of the Major "Western Religions:" Judaism Christianity and Islam. New York: Alkebu-lan Books, 1973.

_____. Black Man of the Nile and His Family: African Foundations of European Civilization and Thought. New York: Alkebu-lan Books, 1973.

_____. A Chronology of the Bible: A Challenge to the Standard Version; a Brief Chronology of the Development and History of the Old and New Testament from its African and Asian Origins of its European and European-American Revisions, Versions, etc. New York: Alkebu-lan Books, 1973.

_____. Our Black Seminarians and Black Clergy Without a Black Theology: The Tragedy of Black People/Africans in Religion Today. New York: Alkebu-lan Books, 1978.

_____, et al. Understanding the African Philosophical Concept Behind the "Diagram of the Law of Opposites." New York: Alkebu-lan Books, 1975.

Budge, E.A. Wallis. The Mummy: Chapters on Egyptian Funeral Archaeology. 2nd ed. New York: Collier Books, 1978.

Carruthers, Jacob H. Essays in Ancient Egyptian Studies. Los Angeles: Timbuktu Publ., 1984.

Chomsky, Noam, and Edward S. Herman. The Washington Connection and Third World Fascism: The Political Economy of Human Rights, Vol. I. Boston: So. End Press, 1979.

Clark, R.T. Rundle. Myth and Symbol in Ancient Egypt. London: Thames and Hudson, 1978.

deGraft-Johnson, J.C. African Glory: The Story of Vanished Negro Civilizations. Baltimore: Black Classic Press, 1986.

deTocqueville, Alexis. Democracy in America, Vol. I. Ed. Phillips Bradley, 1945; rpt. New York: Vintage Books.

Diop, Dr. Cheikh Anta. The African Origin of Civilization: Myth or Reality? Trans. Mercer Cook. Westport: Lawrence Hill and Co., 1974.

_____. Black Africa: The Economic and Cultural Basis for a Federated State. 2nd ed. Trans. Harold J. Salemson. Westport: Lawrence Hill and Co., 1984.

_____. The Cultural Unity of Black Africa: The Domains of Patriarchy and of Matriarchy in Classical Antiquity. 1963; rpt. Introd. by Dr. John Henrik Clarke and Afterword by James G. Spady. Chicago: Third World Press, 1978.

_____. Precolonial Black Africa: A Comparative Study of the Political and Social Systems of Europe and Black Africa, from Antiquity to the Formation of Modern States. Trans. H.J. Salemson. Westport: Lawrence Hill and Co., 1987.

Equiano. Equiano's Travels: The Interesting Narrative of the Life of Olaudah Equiano or Gustavus Vassa the African. 1789; rpt. Ed. P. Edwards. New York: F.A. Praeger, 1966.

Frazer, James G. The New Golden Bough [A Study in Magic and Religion]: A New Abridgement of the classic work. Ed. Theodor H. Gaster. New York: Mentor Books, 1964.

Freud, Sigmund. The Future of an Illusion. Trans. by James Strachey. New York: W.W. Norton, 1961.

_____. Moses and Monotheism. Trans. Katherine Jones. 1939; rpt. New York: Vintage Books.

Galbraith, J. Kenneth. The Affluent Society. 4th ed. New York: Mentor Books, 1985.

Graves, Robert, and Ralphael Patai. Hebrew Myths: The Book of Genesis. Garden City, N.Y.: Doubleday and Co., 1963.

"Headline History." Information Please Almanac. 1987 ed., pp. 105-130.

Hilliard, Asa G., Larry Williams, and Nia Damali, eds. The Teachings of Ptahhotep: The Oldest Book in the World. Atlanta: Blackwood Press, 1987.

Jackson, John G. Introduction to African Civilizations. Introd. by J. Henrik Clarke. Secaucus: Citadel Press, 1974.

James, Dr. George G.M. Stolen Legacy: The Greeks Were Not the Authors of Greek Philosophy, but the People of North Africa, Commonly Called the Egyptians. San Francisco: J. Richardson Assoc., 1976.

Karenga, Maulana. <u>Selections from the Husia: Sacred Wisdom of Ancient Egypt</u>. Los Angeles: Kawaida Publ., 1984.

_____, and Jacob H. Carruthers, eds. <u>Kemet and the African Worldview: Research, Rescue and Restoration</u>. Los Angeles: Univ. of Sankore Press, 1986 (6226 AFE).

Leakey, Richard E., and Roger Lewin. <u>Origins: What New Discoveries Reveal About the Emergence of Our Species and Its Possible Future</u>. New York: E.P Dutton, 1982.

Madhubuti, Haki R. <u>Enemies: The Clash of Races</u>. Chicago: Third World Press, 1978.

Malcolm X. <u>By Any Means Necessary: Speeches, Interviews and a Letter by Malcolm X</u>. Ed. George Breitman. New York: Pathfinder Press, 1980.

_____. Two Speeches by Malcolm X. 2nd ed. New York: Pathfinder Press, 1988.

Mason, Herbert. <u>Gilgamesh: A Verse Narrative</u>. Afterword by John H. Marks. New York: Mentor Books, 1972.

Moore, Shawna. "Interview with Cheikh Anta Diop." Black Books Bulletin, Vol. 4 (Winter 1976), pp. 30-37.

Moyers, Bill. <u>The Secret Government-The Constitution in Crisis</u>. New York: Journal Graphics, 1987.

Nkrumah, Kwame. <u>Class Struggle in Africa</u>. New York: International Publ. Co., 1984.

Piven, Frances Fox, and Richard A. Cloward. <u>Regulating the Poor: The Functions of Public Welfare</u>. New York: Vintage Books, 1972.

Plumpp, Sterling. Black Rituals. Chicago: Third World Press, 1976.

Pritchard, James B. Archaeology and the Old Testament. Princeton: Princeton Univ. Press, 1958.

_____, ed. The Ancient Near East: An Anthology of Texts and Pictures. Princeton: Princeton Univ. Press, 1958.

_____. ed. Ancient Near Eastern Texts Relating to the Old Testament. 3rd ed. Princeton: Princeton Univ. Press, 1969.

Report of the National Advisory Commission on Civil Disorders [The Kerner Report]. Special Introduction Tom Wicker. New York: Bantam Books, 1968.

Robertson, John M. Pagan Christs. New Hyde Park: University Books, 1967.

Rodney, Walter. How Europe Underdeveloped Africa. Revised edition. Introduction by Vincent Harding and Postscript by A.M. Babu. Washington: Howard Univ. Press, 1982.

Rogers, J.A. World's Great Men of Color, Vol. I. Introd. by J. Henrik Clarke. New York: Collier Books, 1972.

_____. Your History from the Beginning of Time to the Present. 1940; rpt. Baltimore: Black Classic Press, 1983.

Smith, Homer W. Man and His Gods. Boston: Little, Brown and Company, 1953.

Snowden, Frank M., Jr. Before Color Prejudice: The Ancient View of Blacks.
Cambridge: Harvard Univ. Press, 1983.

_____. Blacks in Antiquity: Ethiopians in the Greco-Roman Experience. Cambridge: Harvard Univ. Press, 1970.

Sporry, J.T. The Story of Egypt. n.p., n.d.

Staples, Robert. Black Masculinity: The Black Male's Role in American Society. San Francisco: Black Scholar Press, 1984.

Van Sertima, Ivan, and Larry Williams, eds. Great African Thinkers, Vol. I: Cheikh Anta Diop. New Brunswick: Transaction Books, 1987.

Welsing, Frances Cress, M.D. The Cress Theory of Color-Confrontation and Racism (White Supremacy): A Psycho-Genetic Theory and World Outlook. Monograph. Washington, D.C.: Howard Univ., 1970.

Williams, Dr. Chancellor. The Destruction of Black Civilization: Great Issues of a Race from 4500 B.C. to 2000 A.D. Chicago: Third World Press, 1974.

Williams, Eric. Capitalism and Slavery. Introd. D.W. Brogan. London: Andre Deutsch, 1964.

Wilson, William J. The Declining Significance of Race. Chicago: Univ. of Chicago Press, 1978.

Wright, Dr. Bobby. "The Psychopathic Racial Personality." Black Books Bulletin, Vol 2, 1974, pp. 25-31.

_____. The Psychopathic Racial Personality and Other Essays. Chicago: Third World Press, 1985.

Chart A: Dr. Cheikh Diop's Two Cradle Theory

Quality	Southern Cradle (Afrikan)	Northern Cradle (European)
Means of Existence	Agricultural, Settled	Nomadic
Descent	Matriarchy, Matrilineal	Patriarchy, Patrilineal
Gods	One Universal God (e.g., God Amon)	Family, Tribal Gods (e.g., God Yahweh/Jehovah)
Ancestor Worship	Burial	Cremation
Social Traits	Collective, xenophilic, cosmopolitan, peaceful, just, optimistic, moral, idealistic, accepting, equality of the sexes, non-feudal, socialistic	Individualistic, xenophobic, acutely materialistic, destructive, war-like, violent, criminal, oppressive of females, feudal, capitalistic

www.ingramcontent.com/pod-product-compliance
Lightning Source LLC
Chambersburg PA
CBHW070645160426
43194CB00009B/1582